A BILLION FIREFLIES

Critical Conversations
to Shape a New Post-pandemic World

Arun Maira

INDIA • SINGAPORE • MALAYSIA

Notion Press

No.8, 3rd Cross Street,
CIT Colony, Mylapore,
Chennai, Tamil Nadu – 600004

First Published by Notion Press 2021
Copyright © Arun Maira 2021
All Rights Reserved.

Hardcase: 978-1-63850-581-5
Paperback: 978-1-63850-865-6

This book has been published with all efforts taken to make the material error-free after the consent of the author. However, the author and the publisher do not assume and hereby disclaim any liability to any party for any loss, damage, or disruption caused by errors or omissions, whether such errors or omissions result from negligence, accident, or any other cause.

While every effort has been made to avoid any mistake or omission, this publication is being sold on the condition and understanding that neither the author nor the publishers or printers would be liable in any manner to any person by reason of any mistake or omission in this publication or for any action taken or omitted to be taken or advice rendered or accepted on the basis of this work. For any defect in printing or binding the publishers will be liable only to replace the defective copy by another copy of this work then available.

To Shama

Contents

Introduction 9

PART 1

THE CASE FOR CHANGE

Chapter 1   Changing the Paradigm 17

Chapter 2   How Capitalism Corrupted Democracy 25

Chapter 3   Redesigning an Airplane While Flying in It 32

Chapter 4   Global Problems need Small Solutions and
            Systems Thinking 39

PART 2

THE COMPENDIUM

A. THE WORLD 48

    1. 2021: The Time to Act 49

    2. A New Architecture for Global Governance 59

    3. The Software of Democracy 68

    4. Effective Coalitions Form Bottom-Up and Not Top-Down 80

    5. Who Will Robots and Elephants Vote for:
        Donald Trump or Xi Jinping? 85

- 6. Who Do Economists Serve Really? 106
- 7. Why Is Economic Theory behind the Curve? 121
- 8. The Gap between GDP and the SDGs 124
- 9. Movements of Change 128
- 10. Transforming Systems Is Key to Policy Gains 135
- 11. Engineering a Governance System 139
- 12. Keep Older People Engaged, Don't Isolate Them 142

B. INDIA 145

- 1. My Vision for India 146
- 2. Fast Forward India: The People Make the Difference 150
- 3. India: Many Million Fireflies Now 167
- 4. Letter to The Prime Minister, Dr. Manmohan Singh, Published in The Hindu, in May 2009 174
- 5. Flotilla Advancing 178
- 6. India: A Slow Learning Country? 191
- 7. The Great Scramble of Indians to Board India's Economic Bus 194
- 8. The Poor State of the Indian State 197
- 9. Listen to the Voices of the Less Powerful 201
- 10. The Listening Deficit 204
- 11. Fix the Process of Reforming Policies 207
- 12. Recoupling the Economy with Society 210

C. TECHNOLOGY AND BUSINESS 218

    1.   Will Technology Destroy Democracy? 219

    2.   A Business Redesign to Make Capitalism More Inclusive 227

    3.   'Shares' versus 'Values' Conflict in Business 230

    4.   Some Questions About the Ugly Side of Charity 234

    5.   Gandhi not Milton Friedman 237

Acknowledgements 243

Introduction

The Turning Point

The Covid pandemic was a wake-up call. We said—many did—that we will change the world when the pandemic passes. The deaths of so many people with the virus, and the shattering of so many lives in the panic to prevent its spread, had revealed the frailty of economies beneath the sheen of GDP growth. A year later, in 2021, with vaccines rolling out to provide immunity, there is a global sigh of relief. Governments and businesses are eager to get growth back to normal.

What happened to our resolve? We had said we must create a 'new normal'. In fact, even after the financial crisis of 2008, economists wanted to design a new, more resilient, normal in which the economy was not so vulnerable to shocks. The Covid pandemic has made clear they had not. The old normal has gone on. And seems to be returning again.

Large and unanticipated perturbations in systems are symptoms of fundamental instabilities within them. When stock-markets swing wildly, they can blow-up or melt-down. Therefore, speed-breakers are applied to stop them for a while.

More frequent wilder swings in weather patterns around the world are warnings that the Earth's environment is becoming unstable. Therefore, urgent solutions are required to slow down over-exploitation of nature and the pace of climate change.

Frequent economic crises, as well as increases in their amplitudes, are other warnings that global economic growth is unstable. The Asian financial crisis of 1997 affected many countries in East and South East Asia. 15 years later, the global financial crisis in 2008 infected financial institutions around the world. 12 years later, the Covid crisis in 2020 has impacted people's lives everywhere.

Economies of all countries were severely disrupted by the Covid pandemic, poor countries as well as rich ones. Whereas the financial crises harmed institutions and economies, the virus has killed millions of people in many countries, including the world's richest—the USA. In a panic to prevent people catching the infection, they were shut out of their workplaces and locked into their homes for months. Many felt like they were trapped in an air-raid that would not stop. Some refused to stay in, in spite of the danger. Many have been defying their governments and breaking out.

The Covid pandemic was yet another wake-up call that we cannot carry on the way we have been. We must change the 'theories-in-use' in the backs of our heads that are guiding the human caravan on its journey of progress. We must re-examine the fundamentals of economic theories and look into architectural weaknesses in systems of governance.

The lockdowns had a silver lining. They provided time for introspection. The internet proved a boon. Locked-in, people could connect with others locked in wherever they were. Conversations proliferated over the internet.

Like many people, I found myself busier than before, listening to more people in a month sometimes than I had in six months before the lockdown. I observed patterns in the conversations. Some, especially those on WhatsApp groups, were more mere chatter. Others were the usual seminars and panel discussions, of which there were many more now because it was much easier to convene people around the world virtually than it had been when people had to travel to come together.

Given the time and the opportunity, I found myself participating in many conversations with many people I had not met before. There were some older people like me, reflecting on what had gone wrong and what we could do to make things right even so late in our lives. There were also many much younger people setting out into the world to create movements for change. They give me immense hope that, with new ideas, for which they were searching, they would shape a better world.

The flavors of the discussions varied. On one side, the chattering about the events of the day, and complaints, increased. On another, conversations went deeper. In these deeper reflections, people began to examine what had gone wrong to bring us to this crisis. Voices who had been warning before that we cannot carry on in the way we were, and which were not heard amidst the hustle and bustle before the pandemic, were heard more clearly now.

A few weeks into the pandemic, many people seemed to agree that we must not slip from relief to recovery when the pandemic passes. We must "build back better". We must create a "new normal" and a "new economy". They recalled some ideas that had been around already, to make economic growth more resilient, more environmentally sustainable, and more inclusive and just. However, they were ideas on the fringes of public discourse—the impractical ideas of 'idealists'. The time had come to make the ideal the real.

These were ideas about a new score-card for economic progress; systems thinking in place of siloed solutions; networks of small enterprises instead of large organizations; local solutions to spur global change; more compassion and cooperation to rein in destructive competition; and more ethics in innovation and technology.

After the long lock-down, and with hope lit up now with new vaccines, an impatience to get back into business is in the air. Plans are being put forth by economists, governments, and business leaders. Worryingly, many seem just like the old ways. It seems very difficult to unlearn the theories we have relied on so far.

However, it is imperative we find new solutions. Otherwise, another economic and humanitarian crisis may be upon us soon; and it could be even larger next time.

I have been writing in journals for twenty years what I have been learning about fundamental change in the ideas and forms of institutions that are guiding economic progress, and also about how to bring them about. I have written several books too, such as *"Shaping the Future: Aspirational Leadership in India and Beyond" (2002)*, *"Transforming Capitalism:*

Improving the World for Everyone" (2008), *and "Transforming Systems: Why the World Needs a New Ethical Toolkit" (2019).* The lock-down gave me time to reflect and write some more. My friends urged me to speak up more for those millions being left behind by the juggernaut of economic growth, in which the wealth of those at the top has been increasing fast and the lives of those below are becoming more precarious. Even during the pandemic, when millions of lives were shattered, the wealthy became even richer, as Oxfam reported in its annual scorecard of inequality. It presented it to the powerful and wealthy leaders assembled for their annual gathering of the World Economic Forum. (They could not meet in the salons of the Davos ski-resort this year and met instead on the internet).

We must learn to listen more deeply to others around us. We must find common ground. We must listen to our own hearts. What do we care about most, deep down?

Part 1 of this book is a record of insights that emerged from conversations during the lock-down. Part 2 is a compendium of contours of solutions proposed by those who had their ears to the ground before the pandemic and could hear the rumblings beneath it. The compendium is divided into three sections. The first on theories and ideologies driving economic growth globally, including in India. The second is focused more on India. The third is on technology and business. Some are longer essays, and some are shorter op-eds. They include scenarios of India's future prepared by concerned citizens in 2000 using the generative scenario planning process. And also, recent critiques by Noble laureates of the discipline of economics.

My book does not provide any grand solution. Because that is not how the changes the world needs can be, or should be, brought about. Different countries, and different regions within countries, have different problems, and different possibilities. Therefore, local solutions are required, designed and implemented cooperatively by the people living in their own countries, in their own cities, and in their own village communities. However, while devising their own solutions, they must also understand how their actions, for their own good, will nurture, or harm, the conditions of the environment and the broader society around them.

I hope some ideas in this book will provide seeds for conversations amongst concerned people to develop innovative solutions for changing the trajectory of economic progress before it is too late.

PART 1

THE CASE FOR CHANGE

Chapter 1

Changing the Paradigm

The Covid pandemic shut down the world in 2020. In panic, 'social distancing' was enforced everywhere. The Indian government imposed a total lock-down of the entire country. Harsh measures to stop the virus spreading had unforeseen consequences for economies and they harmed the well-being of people more than the virus did.

The most vulnerable people, economically and socially, were hit hardest: not as much by the virus, as by collapse of their precarious incomes and inadequacies of their habitations. Millions spilled out onto the roads in India looking for food and shelter. The mass migration was described as the largest ever in India, exceeding the tragic migrations when the country was partitioned in 1947. Meanwhile around the world, including in India, stock markets hit record highs. The wealth of those most well-off increased, while the poor suffered the most everywhere.

The global lock down was an unplanned 'stress-test' of the structures of economies. Like engineers' stress tests in wind-tunnels of the designs of their airplanes, the lock-down revealed structural weaknesses in economies. It was a wake-up call for policy makers. It enabled introspection. People reached out to each other on the internet. A new world of webinars, zoom meetings, and social media groups mushroomed. People found time to listen to many more people than they used to. And also, time to listen to what they cared about most within themselves.

The first response to the pandemic arose from fear—to protect ourselves. Then came compassion to give relief to those suffering the most. The stress test highlighted the flaw in economic measures, such as GDP, for measuring all-round societal well-being. 'Never again', people swore. We must not return to the 'old normal': we must create a 'new normal'. Even as they rushed to provide relief, people seemed determined that, after the pandemic passes, we would not 'build back' economies in their old forms. Rather, we would build new, more resilient, and more just, economies.

That is what we were thinking then, when we struggled through the unexpected shattering of many lives. The question is: what were we thinking before the pandemic? What are the economic theories that put our societies into these vulnerable conditions? What beliefs was the 'old normal' of good policies built upon? We must examine them because those beliefs had translated into the designs of policies and institutions which have created great vulnerabilities for millions of people beneath a veneer of economic growth. The world seems to be breathing a sigh of relief, with vaccines rapidly rolling out around the world to enable the world to get back to normal. We must pause, before we rush into economic recovery, and critically inquire whether or not the solutions for economic recovery being lined up are, once again, founded on old theories of economics which, we now know, must change.

Sixty years ago, Thomas Kuhn explained in *The Structures of Scientific Revolutions* why embedded beliefs are very hard to change even when new scientific evidence shows they are wrong. Powerful institutions are built upon wide-spread "theories-in-use". The high priests of these ideas will defend the theories because they want to stay on their public pedestals. The political rulers they advise, who use their advice to justify their policies, will also defend them. Ideas and institutions built upon those ideas create a 'paradigm', as Kuhn explained. It is inevitable that an action to change a paradigm will invite a reaction to the change. It is a law of physical systems, and also a law of social systems.

Every system is perfectly designed to produce the results it is presently producing, said Donella Meadows, a doyen of systems thinking. Therefore, if we want very different outcomes, then the design of the system must be changed. To bring about a new normal after the pandemic passes, we must look into the embedded ideas that were driving economic policies before the pandemic struck.

Katherine Boo throws light on these in *Behind the Beautiful Forevers: Life, Death and Hope in a Mumbai Undercity,* which won the National Book Award,

USA, for the best non-fiction book in 2012. "These continual human losses are taken mostly in a matter-of-fact way in Annawadi. For Abdul and his friends have 'accepted' the basic truths: that in a modernizing, increasingly prosperous city, their lives were an embarrassment best confined to small spaces, and their deaths would matter not at all".

On 24th March 2020 India's Prime Minister announced another bold decision as he likes to, and with a mythological metaphor also. With only a few hours' notice, he ordered all Indians not to cross the 'Lakshman Rekha'. They must not step out of the doors of their homes, and they must maintain 'social distances' of two meters from each other. When millions were compelled to break out of the Lakshman Rekha, spilling onto the streets from their tiny, cramped homes, to join long lines of people waiting for food to be doled out to them, an awareness of 'the small spaces' in which millions lived in Indian cities (if they were lucky to have even these rather than sleeping in the streets as many homeless do), hit home to 'people like us', who had been enjoying the fruits of growth of India's GDP within our sheltered enclaves.

Some of the millions thrown out of work and their cramped shelters asked, "What was the Prime Minister thinking of when he made his dramatic announcement? Was he not aware how many millions of the country's citizens live?" reports Harsh Mander in *Locking Down the Poor: The Pandemic and India's Moral Center.*

When I returned to Mumbai in 2000, after ten years in the USA, where I had gone in 1989 before the bold 'liberal market' reforms of 1991 nudged by the IMF (to whom the Indian government was compelled to turn for emergency support), I noticed a vibrancy in the Indian economy. The city's streets were crowded with many models of cars—Honda, Toyota, Mercedes, Audi, BMW, and others too. When I lived in Mumbai in 1989, all one saw on the streets were clunky, Indian made Ambassadors and Premiers, and many new, little Marutis. Hardly any of those old cars had air-conditioning. All the new models I saw in 2000, even the tiny ones, were air-conditioned, which was a relief in Mumbai's sweltering climate. While waiting at traffic lights in Mumbai's notorious traffic jams at least one could keep cool with the windows turned up and the air-conditioner on. I soon noticed a new, ubiquitous, sound in the city that I had not heard before. It was the sound of a knocking on car windows.

Mumbai had slums and beggars in 1989 when I had moved to the USA. There were around now too. In 1989 beggars would approach cars when the traffic stopped and put their hands through the windows. One could drop a coin in their hand or push the hand away. Now, with car windows turned up, one could leave their hands out, and even shut the poor out of mind. They had to knock hard on windows to even be noticed.

Boo writes that the people in the slums she writes about are not counted as 'poor' in official statistics. They are 'among roughly 100 million Indians freed from poverty since 1991' when the central government embraced economic liberalization, she says. The liberation of markets was supposed to provide opportunities for all citizens, not only rich ones, to earn more.

Slum Dog Millionaire, an award-winning movie, was a celebration of one such motivated and resourceful individual from a Mumbai slum, who was rewarded with personal wealth. Such stories let wealthy people off the hook of responsibility for the condition of millions of poor people who lived miserable lives while they struggled to "stand up and start up". This is another one of the Indian Prime Minister's exhortations to Indian citizens who, he says, should not be "job seekers but job creators". It shifts the responsibility for the condition of poor people onto the poor themselves. If they cannot make it, it is because of a lack of spunk in them, and not because the state has not created the conditions for them to earn enough from their tiny ventures, and to live in dignity even if they cannot.

"It is their fault, and not our responsibility" is the attitude of the rich, and even the rising middle class, towards less well-off citizens in a free market economy. This is a "virus of indifference" which has been spreading further in India alongside the growth of GDP facilitated by liberal market reforms. A symptom of the virus is the indifference to the knocking on the window. This virus has been spreading around the world with neo-liberal economics, says Michael J. Sandel in his book, *The Tyranny of Merit: What's Become of the Common Good.*

People who have been suffering from the ill-effects of financial, free market globalization, have knocked hard before. After the global financial crisis of 2008, they went right up to Wall Street. The Occupy Wall Street movement spurred many other Occupy movements in financial centers around the world. The governments of the G-7 countries met, and expanded into the G-20, to take coordinated action for a global recovery. However, their efforts were focused mostly and, in public perception entirely, on the recovery of global GDP and on saving "too big to fail" corporations and financial institutions. They were not concerned about changing the structures of economies so that the incomes and lives of ordinary people would not be vulnerable to economic shocks again. Though economists talked about the need for a "new normal", the "old normal" of economics continued. They only rearranged the deckchairs on the ship, while the Titanic sailed on to the next disaster, which it struck with the Covid pandemic.

It is very difficult to change an embedded paradigm, as Kuhn said. Inequalities continued to increase in spite of (or because of?) the G-20's recovery strategy. The wealthy became even wealthier. The poor became more vulnerable. They also began to realize that the ideas of the experts who were advising their governments were the cause of their problems. A wave of resentment built up against experts and against economists out of touch with the common people. Prime Minister Modi, in another of his aphorisms, said, "India needs less Harvard and more hard work". Brexit; Bernie Sanders and Trump; the rise of authoritarian leaders in democracies, including in India—these were all symptoms of the resentment. Some populist movements against the Establishment took rightward turns, other leftward.

What Are Governments and Experts Thinking of Now?

That is what we were thinking of before the pandemic. What are we thinking of now when governments are focusing on economic recovery?

Before the pandemic, the Prime Minister and his advisers in the NITI Aayog (the national institution for transforming India) with which he had replaced the Planning Commission, had announced that India would, very soon, reach the $5 trillion milestone on its march pf progress. Now, economists within and outside the Indian government, and in the IMF, who are advising it, are debating how soon growth of GDP will get back on track to make India a $5 trillion economy.

Hearing policymakers and business leaders salivating at the prospect of a $5 trillion GDP, I am reminded of a cartoon by R.K. Lakshman. Every morning Lakshman brought to readers of the Times of India the "Common Man's View", in a cartoon on its front page. This cartoon was in the early years of the millennium when "India was Shining" according to the government in power then, with the opening of the economy and stock markets rising. Lakshman's cartoon showed a beggar on a street reading to another beggar from a newspaper with the headline "Economy". "Terrific progress", he exclaims! "In growth rate, in industry, in exports, and in exchange reserves—what a change from the miserable situation we are in!"

Before it was disbanded in 2014, the Planning Commission's last two 5-year plans, were dedicated to 'faster, inclusive, and sustainable growth'. However, the opening chapters of the plans, which gave an overview of the economy, were almost entirely an analysis of trends of economic growth. The deteriorating condition of the environment, and what life was like for Lakshman's 'common man', to whom the benefits of growth were not trickling down, received only passing references amidst the decimal-point analysis of GDP growth.

NITI Aayog, which replaced the Planning Commission, was supposed to make a paradigm shift in planning. However, it has turned out to be mostly old wine in a new bottle. The economic philosophies have hardly changed. What we measure is what we manage, is an aphorism of good management. Modi's advisers were, once again, using GDP as the supreme measure of the country's progress—onwards to $5 trillion! Economic growth is necessary for India no doubt, to provide more opportunities for people to earn incomes. However, what matters to the common man on the ground is the pattern of the growth, and how fast he will be included in it. For him, the economic strategies adopted for growth matter more than the growth of the GDP.

Mr. Modi's government has focused hard to improve India's position in the World Bank' Ease of Doing Business rankings. India has climbed a remarkable 79 rungs during Mr. Modi's watch, and was ranked 63rd of 190 countries in 2019 (when the World Bank suspended its rankings because there were complaints about its accuracy and utility). Meanwhile, other international agencies rank India 179 out of 180 countries in air-quality, 120 out of 122 in water quality, and 94 out of 107 in the global hunger index. Investors' ease of doing business has improved. But ease of living for the common man has not.

The word 'socialist' was added by an amendment to India's Constitution in 1976, to emphasize social and economic equality for all citizens, rich and poor, in India's progress. 'Socialism' became a bad word after the fall of the Berlin Wall and the triumph of the Anglo-Saxon version of private markets, financial capitalism, and anti-government-ism. Socialist governments in Europe were persuaded to follow the US and to become more capitalist. In India too, where economic reformers wanted the country to join the US-led global bandwagon, socialism became bad and capitalism good.

Prime Minister Modi defended capitalism in India's Parliament in February 2021 when the national budget was discussed. There were concerns about the direction the government would give to the country's economic recovery. Would it press on the accelerator for more private sector led development, reducing the role of government? Or would it focus on building the base of the economic pyramid with more government investments in public health, education, and universal social security? In the event, Modi strongly supported "wealth creators". He was not referring to the tiny entrepreneurs in slums struggling to create wealth for themselves. He was defending large corporations against whose wealth and political power rumblings have increased.

"We must first create wealth before it is distributed", liberal economists say. Modi echoed them. In this ideology, the richest people must become even richer so that there is enough for everyone to share. It is the "old normal" thinking. It diverts attention from how the "distribution", supposedly by some "invisible hand", will happen and when. Such "trickle down" economics has not been working. In fact, as Thomas Piketty has painstakingly documented in *Capital in the Twenty-First Century*, the pace of "flow up" of wealth, facilitated by global capitalism, has exceeded the pace of "trickle down" creating even more inequality in the last thirty years. In this view of capitalism, the primary role of government is to make it easier for rich people and large corporations to make more money. The rest will be taken care of by an invisible hand.

Prime Minister Modi was speaking in Parliament against a backdrop of protests by Indian farmers who had besieged the capital demanding the government withdraw laws for reforming agriculture which were forced onto the country without even discussing them in the Parliament. The government said the reforms would free up markets and enable farmers to get better prices and higher incomes. The farmers protested that the reforms were actually intended to let large corporations into India's agriculture sector so that they could make more profits. They worried that large capitalists would squeeze small farmers. (Hence Modi's defense of "wealth creators"). The farmers' principal protest was against the undemocratic way in which the reforms were forced onto the country. In their defense of democracy, they were joined by many civil society organizations in India and other countries.

Chapter 2

How Capitalism Corrupted Democracy

The stand-off in Indian agriculture reforms has become a battle between capitalism and democracy, the two ideologies that were the winners of the Cold War against the communist, totalitarian, Soviet Union. In the US too, the ideology of Wall Street capitalism has been clashing with 'socialist' ideas propounded by Bernie Sanders and other progressive members of the Democratic party since the financial crisis in 2008. Modi was defending capitalist wealth-creators during a debate about the post-pandemic recovery budget of the government of India. In the US, the Congress and Senate are struggling to reconcile conflicting demands of progressive democrats and conservative capitalists in the government's post-pandemic recovery package.

Francis Fukuyama had declared upon the demise of the Soviet Union that the history of ideologies had ended. He said the US-led ideology, of capitalist markets combined with electoral democracy, had finally won. However, the ideological struggle has not ended. In fact, it is the two winners of the ideological war who are now skirmishing with each other around the world—in India and the US, and also in Chile, Brazil, Poland, France, Greece, Italy, South Africa, and other countries.

Institutions are vehicles developed by humans to enable humanity to realize its higher aspirations. Designs of new forms of institutions, such as the limited liability company, have enabled capitalism to expand and, with the evolution of institutions for governing international finance and international trade, to smoothly cross national borders. Capitalist institutions have enabled global and national GPDs to increase, and to lift millions of people out of economic poverty.

Democracy too has evolved over the last three centuries with the designs of institutions such as the parliamentary system, and, in the last century, with the creation of multinational institutions, such as the United Nations and the International Court of Justice, to promote human rights. Institutions of democracy have enabled people—the poor, women, and minorities—who could not have done so one hundred years ago, to participate more visibly in the governance of their societies.

Democracy and capitalism are founded on different conceptions of fundamental rights. Capitalism's foundation is property rights. Democracy's is human rights. Capitalist institutions run on the principle that whosoever owns something has the right to use it as he wishes, and also that whosoever owns more of a shared resource must have a greater say in how that resource is used. Therefore, whoever owns more shares in a corporation has a larger vote than those who own fewer shares. On the other hand, ownership of property does not matter while assigning voting rights in democratic institutions. Because, in democracy, every living person, whether she has a billion dollars of wealth, or no dollars at all, has an equal vote in the governance of the collective human enterprise.

The clash between capitalism and democracy is a clash of fundamental principles for good governance of societies. Just as when appliances designed to run on AC power are plugged into sockets providing DC power, there will be blow-outs, when institutions of governance designed to run on fundamentally different principles are plugged into each other something will blow up.

The Gathering Storm

Economists promoting free markets gained more power within Anglo-Saxon governments from the 1970s onwards. Milton Freedman, famous for his dictum that 'the business of business must be only business', and Frederik Hayek, with his thesis that more government was 'the road to serfdom', persuaded Margaret Thatcher in the UK and Ronald Reagan in the US to push back against governments in their countries and to privatize public services. Reagan even said that Government is not the solution; rather, Government is the problem.

This turn of ideology gave big capital greater power. Democratic governments, as mentioned before, must represent the interests of all people, rich and poor equally. And though the richest people within any society will always be numerically less than the numbers of poorer people (it is a mathematical distribution as the Italian economist Vilfred Pareto had pointed out in the 19th century), the fewer rich will acquire greater power in the governance of societies when the principle of property rights dominates.

The shift in the balance between democracy and capitalism towards capitalism in the last thirty years is made vivid by the creation of international tribunals who adjudicate in disputes between foreign investors in countries and the governments of those countries. Governments of countries, even when they are not democratically elected, represent the interests of millions, even billions, of people in their countries. The other side in the dispute is a few investors of capital. Governments of countries have become to pander too much to financial investors, making it easy for them to enter and exit countries when they will, and to do business anywhere.

The rules of globalization of financial markets and corporate trade have made life much easier for migrant capital than they have for migrant workers. The word 'reform' has taken on a one-way connotation: reforms imply removal of constraints on investors and businesses. This was starkly revealed in India and elsewhere too with the pandemic. The poor lost incomes and homes, while stock markets broke records making investors even richer. The Indian government's shocking move at the same time, for 'reforming' labor laws to attract more foreign investments by making it easier for employers to fire workers, and curb their unions, made clear who had political power. Power was with large investors and corporations, not with workers and common people.

Western civilizational ideas were declared the victors when the Cold War ended. When Mahatma Gandhi had been asked half a century earlier what he thought of Western civilization, he had replied, tongue in cheek, that it would be a good idea. Gandhi was not a fan of the Soviet regime. According to him both systems—the Soviet state system and the

Western capitalist system—took power away from people on the ground to people up there, remote from them. In the Soviet model, power was in the hands of bureaucrats who ran so-called 'public' enterprises in which the people were merely workers doing what they were paid to and told to. In the Western model, the power was in the hands of owners of, honestly labelled, 'private' enterprises, in which too the workers must do what they are paid to and told to. In the Soviet model, the surplus created by their work moves upwards into the state's coffers. In the capitalist model, the profits move to private owners. In both cases, wealth flows from the bottom to the top.

No fan of Soviet socialism or Western capitalism, Gandhi advocated new models of enterprises in which the workers, the real wealth-creators, would earn wealth for themselves. He advocated reforms of economic institutions whereby producers would not have to pass on all wealth to people above them with the hope that it will somehow, at some time in the future, trickle down to them.

Gandhi understood very well that political freedom, with only the right to elect one's own government, is an incomplete freedom. All citizens must also have economic and social freedoms, he insisted. They must have access to opportunities to earn more, and in a dignified manner, and to accumulate more wealth for themselves.

The world needs better institutions for governance of humanity's economic, social, and political progress. These institutions must also care for the natural systems of the planet on which everyone depends. The hope of many is that we will not waste the crisis of the pandemic of 2020, and that it will spur us to get out of the ruts of our old thinking that has brought us to our civilizational crisis. Reforms of socio-economic governance systems are overdue. A new phase in the histories of ideologies and institutions will emerge with the combination of the principles of capitalism and democracy in the designs of new institutions at many levels. Multi-lateral institutions like the WTO need fundamental reforms. At the national level, people's voices must be heard by national governments over the voices of large corporations. On the ground, new forms of "social enterprises" are required which will enable small producers to become wealth-creators too.

An Infectious Ideology From West to East

The Covid virus spread around the world, East to West, from Wuhan in China. The neo-liberal ideology infecting governance systems has spread the other way, from West to East.

When he was asked for his views on businessmen who created wealth, Gandhi said he had no problem with business wealth-creators. However, they must realize, he said, that they are society's trustees of the wealth their businesses create. They must keep only a little for themselves and use the rest for society's well-being. Gandhi's moral question, "Wealth-creators for whom?" was lost in the new calculus of wealth. Economics and business management became mired in a conceptual confusion, assuming that the cashier who receives the money in the till is the creator of the wealth and deserves to take a large share of it.

I left India in 1989 before the Indian economy was 'liberated' by the big-bang reforms, of 1991. These were guided by the Washington Consensus. The consensus was that less regulation by government and more freedom for private enterprises was good for everybody. Those governments whose policies were designed to care for the most disadvantaged in their societies, as many European governments were, were dismissed as backward 'socialists'. The Indian government, which had gone so far as to add the word 'socialist' in its Constitution, clearly needed to become more capitalist according to the Washington Consensus.

I joined a management consulting company in the US. Business values were changing too. The mantra that "the business of business must be only business", propounded by Milton Friedman of the Chicago School of Economics, was changing the orientation of business management. Friedman's ideas had also inspired Thatcher and Reagan to push back governments to give more freedom to the animal spirits of capitalists. Production of share-holder value became the sole purpose of a business enterprise; and societal and environmental concerns became externalities in the management calculus.

The 1990s also coincided with the technology boom, when the internet—a global public enterprise—was monetized by private entrepreneurs in

Silicon Valley. Young technology geeks, freshly out of college, and some who had not even graduated, became billionaires. Management consulting companies were both stimulators and beneficiaries of the tidal waves of "innovation" in technology, business models, and economic reforms.

Management consultants helped corporations to maximize shareholder value with smart financial engineering, by downsizing, acquiring, and merging their balance sheets with others. In the process employees were removed or dislocated, and communities were impacted too when businesses shifted. Venture capitalists aimed for fast exits after multiplying their investments many times over, moving onto other 'in-and-out' investments to multiply their wealth further. They were creating 'value', they said. However, it seemed to be value only for the shareholders, while the value created for society was unclear.

When the wealth a person garners for himself, and shows off too, becomes the measure of his worthiness, value systems are corrupted. The race amongst entrepreneurs and CEOs to the top of wealth rankings accelerated in the business world. Forbes and other business magazines published annual rankings of the wealthiest individuals and highest paid CEOs. How much money one had made, and how soon, became the measures of personal success.

Left Liberals and Right Liberals

Individual freedom is the core of liberal philosophy. It requires liberty for all humans to stand up, speak up, and form associations to represent their collective interests. Liberals on both sides—'left' and 'right'—are united on this much: all persons must have liberty to stand up, speak up, and form associations in the political sphere. On this they stand united against authoritarian governments who suppress civil liberties. Where they differ is on the rights of individuals to exercise their liberties within economic institutions.

Leftward liberals demand that workers must have the right to speak up and form associations to defend their liberties and these rights must extend against investors in business institutions too. For rightward liberals, civic liberties stop at the walls of their institutions. They would deny workers the right to exercise their civil liberties and to form unions for representing their collective interests within business institutions.

When the Soviet Union collapsed, an advocate for workers' rights in the US observed that the last remaining totalitarian state was the Western, capitalist, business corporation.

Tendencies towards fascism, and crony capitalism too, arise from a convergence of capitalists' and anti-democratic governments' beliefs that democratic forces must be suppressed to enable efficient governance of enterprises.

Chapter 3

Redesigning an Airplane While Flying in It

Institutions are the vehicles in which society travels and progresses, economists admit. When the financial policies they had recommended, caused economic crises in many Asian countries in the 1990s, IMF's economists declared the flaw was not in their policies: it was in weaknesses in the countries' institutions.

Douglass C. North received the Nobel Prize in economics in 1993 for his work on the development of institutions and their role in human progress. North defined institutions as 'the humanly devised constraints that structure political, economic and social interactions'. Constraints, he said, are devised as formal rules (constitutions, laws, property rights) and informal restraints (sanctions, taboos, traditions, codes of conduct). North explained that institutions are not just the 'hard' stuff—the buildings of courts and parliaments. Nor are they just the written down constitutions and laws which keep lawyers busy. The essence of institutions lies in the norms and values of people in their societies. People demand new laws and policies when societal norms and values change. Laws for universal franchise, affirmative action for women and minorities, and universal social security, were outcomes of changing social values and movements for change.

When I returned to India in 2000, after eleven years in the USA, stock markets were booming in India, as they were elsewhere in the world. The 3% of Indians who could afford some investments in the stock market were feeling much richer. The business media began to devote more space to happenings in the stock market and less to the lives of the remaining 97% of Indians.

When I left India in 1989, it was not fashionable to show off one's wealth. When I returned in 2000, India's largest newspaper, The Times of India, had a new page in it—"page 3"—which reported the parties the rich had attended in 5-star hotels, and who was seen with whom, the expensive clothes they wore, and even the luxury cars they arrived in for the party.

I was happy to note, however, that The Times of India continued to carry R. K. Lakshman's iconic cartoon, "The Common Man's View". It was a daily reminder to the paper's readers about the realities of India: a little knocking on the window of the consciousness of Indian citizens which was sadly getting lost in the news of economic growth.

I remember one cartoon very well. It showed two beggars at the bottom of the stairs to the Bombay Stock Exchange. Two, fat, dhoti-clad, stockbrokers are coming down the stairs, laughing happily. One beggar turns to the other with a big smile. "Look, we are really fortunate—the Sensex must have gone up still further!", he says.

The Economic Times, the Times of India's associate newspaper which focuses on economics, the business sector, and the stock market, invited me to write my views in a monthly column. Four years later, Sage Publications suggested I publish my articles in a book, *Remaking India: One Country, One Destiny*. Worried that readers would find a collection of newspaper articles too dry, and because a picture can say more than a thousand words, I obtained Mr. Lakshman's permission to use some of his cartoons to amplify my prose.

The book included the cartoon with the beggars beneath the stock exchange hoping for the trickle down of a little wealth to them. Another cartoon showed a government minister, who has arrived in his car in a rural area, surrounded by villagers bowing before him with folded hands. He berates them: "All the time you keep asking for drinking water. Don't you ever want to progress? I am giving you telephones?" The cartoon was Lakshman's comment on the lop-sidedness of India's economic growth which benefitted the rich much more than the poor. Even now, defenders of the 1991 reforms cite how long it took to get a telephone connection before the reforms when telephony was the monopoly of public sector enterprises. Meanwhile, even today, millions in city slums continue to wait in long lines for cans of water, and women in rural India continue to walk miles to fetch water for their homes.

The BJP-led NDA government, which was governing India then, was celebrating India's economic progress. It ran an international campaign declaring that "India is Shining'. However, its' campaign backfired in India, and it lost the elections in 2004. A Congress-led UPA government came to power. Sonia Gandhi, the leader of the Congress Party, was credited with the victory. She had connected with the common people, sounding often like her mother-in-law, the redoubtable 'socialist', Indira Gandhi, who with her cry of 'garibi hatao' (remove poverty) had won the hearts of India's masses in the 1970s. She had also inserted the word 'socialism' into the Constitution of India in 1976.

In a surprise move, Sonia Gandhi nominated Dr. Manmohan Singh as the Prime Minister. This was a big relief for India's capitalists. Manmohan Singh was lauded by them as the big reformer of the Indian economy in 1991, when he was finance minister and big liberal market reforms were made. Their freedoms would not be curbed, and indeed they counted on more freedoms from his government.

During its first tenure from 2004 to 2009, Dr. Manmohan Singh's government was constrained in making much further 'pro-capitalist' reforms by the Left parties whose support the Congress had needed to form the government. In 2009, the Congress won enough seats to be able to form a government without the Left parties in it. This time, the corporate lobbies expected more from him.

Economic growth continued upwards with the new government. However, listening for the knocking on windows as I was, it was clear that the growth was coming at great cost to the environment, and also was not improving the well-being of a large proportion of the Indian people. I continued to write my views in Indian journals.

When Dr. Manmohan Singh became Prime Minister for his second term. I took courage to write an open letter to the Prime Minister in The Hindu on 26th May 2009, I cautioned him not to yield to corporate pressures until corporations reformed themselves. They must act more responsibly towards society and the environment—to become a little more 'socialist' and a little less 'capitalist', perhaps. I wrote:

"Dr. Manmohan Singh, the time has come for you, your government, and India, to make a seminal contribution to the world. You have the mind and the heart to do this. Dr. Singh, now that you do not need the support of the Left parties, Indian business leaders are clamouring for you to implement their reform agenda. These are the same reforms—to reduce government involvement and open up more sectors for investment—that they had asked from your previous government. A hint that you may do so makes the stock market soar. However the philosophy from which these reforms spring—to increase corporate investments and profits, and GDP—is from the same school of economics that was driving economic policies in countries in the West that are now suffering its consequences.

Dr. Singh, India needs a social and political consensus about the philosophy that will take it to its tryst with destiny. Reform policies must follow from this. Healthy democracies require not just elections. They also require platforms for dialogues to reconcile differences. The democrats of ancient Greece conducted such debates civilly and in public view in city plazas. In India, the Emperors Ashoka and Akbar created councils for dialogue between people with different beliefs. Institutions for public dialogue in the Indian democratic state are not functioning at this time. Parliament now meets less and less, and when it does, its proceedings degenerate into shouting matches and walk-outs. Discussions in our media are set up as 'big fights' for entertainment to attract advertisers. Political differences are being settled on the streets."

Writing a letter to a Prime Minister in a newspaper is vanity. The Prime Minister is not expected to read it. I was startled when a month later Dr. Manmohan Singh invited me to become a Member of the Planning Commission of India which he chaired. I was honoured but I was not sure I was the person he was looking for. I was not an economist, did not have a doctorate in any field, and had no previous experience in the government—one or the other of which qualification seemed to be required for the Planning Commission. I asked him if he was aware that I was not qualified for the responsibility.

He said I was well qualified *because* I did not have the usual qualifications. He said the country needed to refresh its approach to economic growth because the present pattern was not inclusive or environmentally sustainable. The Planning Commission seemed stuck in a rut. Many attempts had been made to reform it over the past thirty years, even by him when he was the Deputy Chairman of the Commission. He was aware of my experience in assisting institutions to reform, and he wanted me to examine how the Planning Commission should be reformed. I would be a full time Member within the Commission, not a consultant outside it. I would have the same duties as other Members in the subjects allotted to me which were policies for industrial development and urbanisation. However, in addition, while experiencing what it was like to work in the Planning Commission, I should recommend how it should be reformed. My task was like redesigning an airplane in which I was flying.

I have written about my experience, and about what I learned about reforms of institutions from experts around the world, in my book, *Redesigning The Aeroplane While Flying: Reforming Institutions* (published in 2014).

The process of institutional reforms is like redesigning an airplane in which one is flying. Institutions, as North explained, are formed by the ways in which people think and behave. Institutions provide guiderails, and stability, in a complex, dynamically changing world. Therefore, people want to hold on to them. Institutional change creates instability and therefore there is resistance within institutions to changing them, and even from around them. Because people like stability and find comfort in what they are used to even if it is not perfect.

Nevertheless, crises can compel people to step out of their comfort zones and risk change. There are two types of crises. One is a "crisis of condition", when the world around changes so much that internal change becomes necessary for survival. This was India's crisis in 1991. Gold from the country's reserves had to be flown out to provide collateral for emergency loans it needed from abroad. The country's economy could not survive in the condition in which it was.

Another type of crisis can also spur change. These are "crises of aspiration". They occur inside minds, and within institutions, when people realise they will not able to reach their aspirational goals if they do not change their institutions. Crises of aspiration can spur innovative changes; and they can prevent crises of condition that would arise in the future if change is not made in time. Aspiration for a vision, which is out of reach with prevalent forms of institutions, demands innovation and change in them. For change to happen many people within and around the institution must have a shared vision of what they want. And they must become prepared to undertake a risky journey of change.

The crisis of condition caused by the pandemic will be wasted unless there is a shared vision of what we want the future to be. The SDGs have provided the contours of a comprehensive vision for all countries, which can be sharpened for their specific requirements by the countries. However, it is not enough to only have a vision of the future outcomes we want. We must also have a shared vision of the process by which we will realize our vision.

When the vision is large and the journey is long, it is necessary to have agreement about how we will govern ourselves during the journey. That is why questions about whether we will follow principles of socialism or capitalism, or democracy or authoritarianism, have become urgent. These are different approaches, with different principles of governance, that enable the coordination and regulation of economic and political activities during the journey.

The criterion for choosing an approach cannot be merely utilitarian, i.e. only an evaluation of which approach will be the most efficient to get the job done. For example, to get a large army across the mountains, an authoritarian approach, ensuring optimum use of the material resources available, may be swiftest to get most of the army and its equipment across. However, other norms can apply too, such as which approach is most fair to all travellers. Should anyone be left behind? And should the weak be discarded on the way because they are a burden for the progress of the rest?

The fundamental question for choosing an inclusive approach to socio-economic change must be what sort of society we want to be, and not how large an economy do we want to have? Societies (and institutions within them) are the means by which we achieve our aspirations of what we want.

Social institutions are not machines composed of mechanical parts wired up by an engineer according to his blue-print. They are living organisms, formed by the interactions of many, diverse, living organisms within them. Our individual lives are *processes*, not objects. Societies too are *processes*, not things. Social and economic institutions are the *means* by which we attain our aspirations. When humans reach one level of aspiration, they look up to the next one. Then another journey must be undertaken through unknown territory. Thus humanity has progressed and thus it will progress further. Humanity's progress is a process of *learning together* to do what human beings have not done before.

When we realise that the airplane in which we are flying together is creaking, and that it must climb much higher to go over the mountain range in its path, we have no option but to redesign it as we are flying in it. We will have to cooperate with each other. The people in the first class cabin cannot be safe if they improve only their part of the airplane. The tail section and the people in it must be safe too or else the whole plane will crash.

We must listen very well to each other if we want to learn together. We must listen to what each of us cares about most of all. We must respect others as we expect they must respect us. The fair principles by which we will govern our interactions while we endeavour to improve the world for ourselves, and for others too, will emerge from these deeper conversations. Dialogues and deliberations amongst people with diverse histories, and diverse needs, and diverse capabilities, are the essence of democracy. From such democratic deliberations, collective visions of goals will emerge, as will pathways to reach them.

Our institutions of capitalism and democracy need reforms to enable us to save humanity from climate change. They also need urgent reforms to enable everyone on our shared planet, rich and poor, to live in dignity and with hope, and to feel an equal citizen in the collective human endeavour.

Chapter 4

Global Problems need Small Solutions and Systems Thinking

The Covid crisis is the story of two global solutions to a medical problem: one was lockdowns; the other, vaccines.

Lockdowns with social distancing were implemented in all countries on the advice of medical experts. They prevented the virus spreading. Lockdowns also had many side-effects from which people suffered greatly. Businesses closed down and people lost incomes. In crowded Indian cities, where poor people had no place to stay locked in, they had to venture out even to fetch water, and were harassed by police enforcing the lockdown. The single-minded focus on the treatment of Covid shut out patients of other ailments from hospitals. Doctors estimated that more people died from lack of treatments they were getting, but could not any longer, than the numbers who were treated for Covid. Closures of schools, even in richer countries, caused concerns about the long-term impacts on the development of children. In many countries—the US, the UK, the Netherlands, and others—citizens ailed by lock-downs, refused to follow the rules, causing law-and-order problems too.

The roll-out of new vaccines is a remarkable story of innovations produced by many scientists and many organizations in many countries. Citizens waited anxiously for the vaccines to become available. However, governments followed protocols established by medical scientists for testing new vaccines very strictly to ensure there would be no side-effects when solutions found in labs were applied to masses of people.

The contrast between how the two solutions were implemented raises important questions: about scale, centralization, and the scientific approach. These must be addressed urgently because humanity has large challenges and needs effective ways to meet them. The Sustainable Development Goals (SDGs) require large scale solutions to be implemented very fast. Because the clock is ticking: the planet is warming, and inequalities are increasing.

The 17 SDGs fall into four groups. Poverty, hunger, health, education, and gender equality relate directly to human development. Water, energy, climate action, life below water, and life on land belong to the environment group. The third group relates to the economy: decent work and economic growth, reduced inequalities, responsible consumption and production, and industry innovation. The fourth group, viz. 'peace, justice and strong institutions', and 'partnerships for growth', provide the rules of conduct amongst stakeholders on humanity's journey to achieve the SDGs.

Problems such as persistent poverty and inequality, poor health, and environmental degradation, that the SDGs aim to solve are systemic issues. They have multiple inter-acting causes. They cannot be solved by any one actor. Nor are they amenable to silver bullet solutions.

The break-down of 'systems thinking' along with remarkable scientific advances has created an epistemic crisis. The problem policymakers (and experts) have in the 21st century is that there are many problems, and *all must be solved simultaneously*. The complexity of the SDGs cannot be simply broken up into pieces to solve. The challenges are interconnected. Solutions to environmental problems that aggravate problems of livelihoods cannot be good solutions. Or solutions to economic problems that aggravate environmental problems. Solutions to increase GDP which also increase inequity will not help to make the world better for everyone.

Scientific advances since the European Enlightenment have multiplied the numbers of specialists. An abundance of experts now available to solve diverse problems should be a blessing. However, their abundance has become a problem because experts are too narrowly focused on separate pieces of the system: they are *not able to comprehend the whole system*. Specialists in diseases of the heart do not understand sufficiently the effects of their interventions on other systems in the human body, and patients must turn to other specialists for treatment of the side-effects of the solution to their heart problems. Often, they end up with a mental health specialist to help them manage their confusion and depression, and their anxiety about the cumulative cost of their wonderful treatments.

The economy, society and ecology are integrated in a system. Changes in any one of these components will affect the others. Components of systems must be in harmony with each other for the system to remain healthy. Lock-downs to prevent Covid are an example of unintended consequences of a good solution which were not foreseen because the whole system was not kept in view.

A property of complex systems is that many good things interacting may unwittingly produce bad outcomes. The epistemic problem is this: experts mentally break complex systems into parts and then try to improve them separately. Thus, economists worry about the economy, and sociologists about society, and ecologists about ecology. And they quarrel with each other. Economists think ecologists are coming in the way of growth. Sociologists say economists do not understand that humans are human beings and not commodities in labour markets.

In the prevalent paradigm of managing complex systems in governments and large corporations, each part of a complex system is managed by specialists reporting up to the top. There, they try to coordinate the whole system. All have their programmes and their budgets and each passes down instructions to its subordinates who are responsible for only parts of the system.

Centralization is the wrong approach for solving complex problems which manifest in different shapes in different places. For example, environmental problems combine with livelihood problems in different ways in the Himalayan mountains in the North of India, in the dry lands of Rajasthan in the middle, and in the lush coastal regions of Kerala in the South. Therefore, *local systems solutions are necessary for such global systemic problems*. The solution is, responsibility for the governance of complex systems must be devolved to communities in their localities. However, not only politicians, also experts at the top, are reluctant to let go of their power. They claim that the locals will not have the capability to manage, and so the centre must take on the burden of managing the locals.

Clearly we cannot carry on the way we are. Therefore we must examine some prevalent beliefs driving models of growth. For one, the paradigm of progress has swung too far towards the global and has forgotten the local. And another, in their drive for 'economies of scale' economists and managers are overlooking the need for 'economies of scope'. Economies of scope emerge when diverse capabilities, even on small scales, are easily accessible to each other, can produce innovations together, and improve the overall performance of the system.

Large global supply chains create economic efficiencies. Food is grown in large farms across the world, each specializing in different vegetables and fruits. However these large global chains consume more energy, cause more damage to the environment, and create more risk than local networks. The average morsel of food eaten by an American travels about 1500 miles from these large farms to reach his fork. On the way, large quantities of oil are burnt for refrigeration and transportation and lots of carbon is spewed into the atmosphere. Such global chains increase other risks too. When bad tomatoes were suspected to be the cause of a salmonella problem in the USA, it was impossible for retailers to pin-point their source. So supplier farms had to be shut down in many places across the world. The 'sub-prime' financial crisis was another example of risks in large interconnected supply chains. The theory was that the financial system would be safer by spreading risky loans across a wider system. However, when things began to go wrong there was panic because it was not clear where the bad bits were hidden!

When Thomas Friedman launched his paean to a global world, *The Earth is Flat: A Brief History of the 21st Century*, in Delhi in 2005, I was invited, along with Mani Shankar Aiyar, Indian cabinet minister for local self-government, to discuss Friedman's book with him at the launch. Aiyar pointed out the flaw in Friedman's thesis. Friedman said the world was flat because he observed that people in Bangalore could now talk to anyone, anywhere in the world. Aiyar retorted that people in Bangalore, while becoming integrated with the world, did not know what was happening in villages just fifty miles away. They were flying around the world connecting with people in New York and London and losing touch with those nearby.

Fashions in Ideas Are Hard to Change

Big is not always better. Ecologists explain how small systems, with diversity within them, have the ability to adapt and evolve. They are more sustainable than large systems. They do not expend too much energy in making connections between their diverse parts. They may not have 'economies of scale' but they have powerful 'economies of scope'. Diversity makes life more interesting also. Thus, life within city neighbourhoods that have their own groceries, cafes, bookshops, and doctors is more pleasant than in cities which are segregated into large zones dedicated for different uses.

Several foresighted people in the last century have suggested that we should look for more local solutions to what have become global problems. In their book, *Winning the Oil Endgame,* published in 2004, Amory Lovins and his colleagues in the Rocky Mountain Institute explained how 'a legion of small, fast and simple microgeneration and efficiency projects' could be the answer to the world's energy problems. In *Deep Economy (2007),* Bill McKibben made a compelling case for local food networks. There are many examples from India and elsewhere that show that local community solutions for water are more effective and sustainable than gigantic storage and long distance transportation schemes. And micro-credit to local women's self-help groups has become a success story of micro-empowerment.

E.F. Schumacher's *Small Is Beautiful: A Study of Economics As If People Mattered*, published in 1973, brought his critiques of mainstream economics to a wider audience. This was when ideas of global economy were gaining strength. Schumacher foresaw "the attendant evils of mass unemployment and mass migration" within the capital-and-technology driven model of economic growth driving globalization, which was being adopted by developing countries too. The evils of mass unemployment and mass migration he had foreseen, and which were not noticed enough under the growth of economies since then, spilled out into India's cities and highways when the lock-down was enforced in 2020.

Mohandas Gandhi was 'vocal for local' because it makes democracy stronger and the economy healthier too. Schumacher was an admirer of Gandhi's ideas.

The world goes round. And ideas relegated to the fringe are attractive again. Both Gandhi and Adam Smith propounded the idea of markets. And both expressed the idea in terms of local and social phenomena, rather than in terms of global commodity and currency markets. Smith's baker and candlestick maker lived in the same village and knew each other. Mahatma Gandhi foresaw the village community as an environmentally and socially sustainable solution to India's needs. Into that interdependent community, in which people would respect each other, he wanted to draw all providers of services, including the village's scavengers. It is unlikely that the concept of the global village will be sustainable if local towns and villages do not thrive.

The roles of problem-solvers in multi-lateral institutions and in national governments must shift, from being expert problem solvers for the people on the ground, to become deep listeners to the people, and supporters of them in finding their solutions.

The internet, which has enabled people around the world to connect with each other, is breaking them apart, into ideological silos—of people who do not like each other or trust each other even though they live right next to each other. Sadly, the world has become "broken into fragments by narrow domestic walls" (in the words of Rabindranath Tagore, who wrote India's national anthem also).

Environmental sustainability, equitable capitalism, and deep democracy are humanity's aspirations in this century. These aspirations are spread across the 17 SDGs. They can be achieved only by local solutions to these global systemic problems. People everywhere must be willing to listen to 'people not like themselves' in their localities because that is where realities are created, not in conferences of global experts.

I end this chapter with the poem with which I opened my book, *Listening for Well-Being: Conversations with People Not Like Us (2017)*.

Listening

It is time to press the pause button;
Put our smartphones on silent.

Shut out the tweets, trolls, and soundbites;
And stop the windmills in our minds.

It is time to listen.

To listen to the whispers in the trees;
To the caring in our hearts.

And most of all, to the voices of
People Not Like Us.

Then we will learn
And find solutions for living together
On our shared Earth.

PART 2

THE COMPENDIUM

A. THE WORLD

1

2021: The Time to Act

It's the time to look back at the year that has passed, and to look ahead to a new one. A time for reflections about regrets and satisfactions; also, the time for new resolutions. "Which are the three best books you read in 2020?" Anil Dharker, the director of the Tata Literature Festival, asked me during a discussion of my book, *The Learning Factory: How the Leaders of Tata Became Nation-Builders*. I took the liberty of offering four.

2020 will be recorded in history as the year the world was upended by the Covid-19 virus. Last December, before the virus had appeared, I had selected two books on economics for the annual ritual of which books would I recommend.

Ever since the previous global economic crisis in 2008, which had been caused by a financial virus that spread around the world from the US, economists have been searching for a 'new normal'—a new theory to explain how economies really function. Last year, in my essay, *Who Do Economists Serve Really?*, I had reviewed two books written by Nobel laureates in economics who pointed to limitations in their professions' knowledge. These were:*Measuring What Counts: The Global Movement for Well-Being* by Joseph Stiglitz (who won the Nobel prize in 2001), Jean-Paul Fitoussi and Martine Durand, and *Good Economics for Hard Times—Better Answers to Our Biggest Problems* by Abhijit Banerjee and Esther Duflo (who won the Nobel prize in 2019).

A core message from these books was that economics, with its enamour for quantification and equations, is unable to appreciate the qualities of human lives and the relationships that shape societal realities.

The shock of Covid-19 in the first months of 2020 stopped economic growth around the world. The fault lines in economies which had been visible for many years before, and to which the Nobel laureates had drawn attention in 2019, became glaringly wide, with the stresses Covid-19 caused. Hundreds of millions of people, who had been precariously holding onto the global growth bandwagon before Covid-19, lost their jobs and incomes. Governments geared themselves up to provide relief. There was anxiety about when economies could be restarted. There was also resolve that, this time, unlike the post financial crisis recovery, economies should not be merely restarted and growth as usual restored. This time, we must create a new, more resilient, and more just, economic architecture.

The long months of lockdown, not yet over at the end of 2020, have provided a gift of time to pause and reflect; to meet many more people than one used to, on Zoom and in webinars because no time was lost in travel; and to read of course—new books as well as some older ones. I asked Anil if my selection of books has to be restricted to books published in 2020. His only condition was that the books should not have gone out of print so that those interested could read them. So I selected four that I found most relevant for the systemic problems that we must solve for creating more resilient economies and a more just society.

Four Systemic and Epistemic Challenges

The variety of systemic challenges for which solutions are essential have been described in the 17 Sustainable Development Goals which were adopted by all countries in 2015. They cover a wide range of environmental, economic, and social issues—climate change, environmental degradation, poverty, inequality, inadequate public health and education, persistent human indignities, etc. All are interrelated. None can be solved in separate silos. Because narrow solutions to some can harm others, e.g. faster growth to solve poverty problems can exacerbate inequalities and environmental degradation as it has, whereas poorer people do need more incomes and count on economic growth to provide them opportunities to earn. Therefore, the 17th SDG emphasises the needs for strong partnerships among stakeholders, and among diverse experts in their fields too, to achieve all the SDGs. They also call for new thinking because, as Albert Einstein is reputed to have said, one cannot solve intractable-seeming problems with the same type of thinking that has caused them.

The shutdown of the Indian economy by Covid-19 provided some relief on the environmental front. Pollution levels reduced, highlighting again that the country's pattern of economic growth is not environmentally sustainable. The shutdown also highlighted four systemic socioeconomic problems that require new solutions. The books I recommend relate to these challenges.

1. Trade, Industry, and Employment

One is the chronic problem of unemployment (and underemployment). Inadequacies of employment and fragilities of incomes were revealed with millions of migrant workers who fell out of the economy as soon as the economic engine stopped. The need for a more robust industrial policy to create more secure employment within the country was highlighted. However, the solution was resisted by trade economists who berated the Indian government, when it hesitated to join the Regional Comprehensive Economic Partnership (RCEP), for 'thinking local' when they felt the country must become 'more global'. Others pointed out that it is a matter of sequencing, and unless enterprises within India become competitive by skilling and employing more people, the country cannot participate equitably in global supply chains.

2. Small and informal enterprises

The chronic problems of the Indian economy, according to mainstream economists, are the large size of the informal sector of the economy and the paucity of large-scale enterprises. They would like to formalise the informal sector quickly and they would like larger enterprises to be formed to create more employment. Whereas, other economists, as well as people who work closer to the ground, point out that informal and small enterprises are essential for spreading around more opportunities for people to climb up the economic ladder from the bottom, and to contribute to the progress of economic growth.

In fact, the informal sector is an essential feature of a resilient economy. It accounts for 60% of the global economy. Within developing countries it is 90%. India is not an outlier. Therefore, rather than looking down upon it, policymakers must listen to it and learn to nurture it, rather than to surgically distort it with schemes to convert its forms.

3. The divide between experts and the common man

Around the world, common people have become mistrustful of experts in public policy who decide what is good for the people—whether they are the EU's experts in Brussels, or India's central planners in Delhi, or federal government experts in Washington. Brexit was English citizens' vote for freedom from Brussels' experts. Indian citizens' mistrust has become poignantly evident in the scenes of farmers camping around Delhi in the bitter winter cold demanding that agricultural reforms devised by the government's scientific advisers must be withdrawn. Experts say the people don't get it. The people say the experts don't understand their realities. Moreover, how can experts in the old 'normal' way of thinking be expected to come up with substantially new solutions, they wonder?

4. The ethics of technology

Technology, especially technology of the digital variety, seems to have become a panacea for almost all problems. Science-based technologies can have transformative impacts in many fields—in health, education, financial services, logistics, etc no doubt. However, they can often have harmful side-effects too, and therefore must be restrained in their applications. This is a challenge whenever transformative technologies are developed.

Nuclear energy—clean and abundant—could have provided an alternative to dirty and exhaustible fossil fuels. However, ever since its discovery, mankind has been struggling to put the genie back in the bottle, to prevent its proliferation. During the extended lockdowns in the Covid pandemic, virtual education seemed to be a good solution. However, it has exacerbated differences between those who have access to digital modes of communication and those who do not. Further, social media, which was supposed to be a means to bring the world together has turned out to be a dangerous divider, spreading hate and propaganda, and forcing people into groups who do not like each other.

Fortunes are often made by private investors in new technologies, as they have been made by investors in the four largest global companies that dominate the internet. Controlling them now has become a huge political problem for governments. When considerations of the public good clash with the pursuit of private profit, the debate is confounded by an ideological belief that interference by governments with a free market, in which people can pursue their private interests, is always bad. The debate divides economists into two camps. On one side are the capitalist free marketers; on the other side the so-called 'socialists'.

It is dawning now that more technology is not the solution. More wisdom is required also to create a more sustainable and equitable new normal.

The Books

Global trade and local markets

The first book on my list, *Empire of Cotton: A Global History*, by Sven Beckert, is a masterly history of global trade and its impact on societies. Beckert, a professor of history at Harvard University and a fellow of the American Council of Learned Societies, has researched the growth of trade in cotton and cotton textiles over many centuries. Cotton-related trade is the most global sector of the global economy touching all countries—all as consumers, a majority as processors of cotton and its textiles, and many, in almost all continents, as growers of cotton. The volume of global trade has been growing consistently, but its patterns have changed.

For example, India was the largest exporter of cotton textiles until the British took over the global trade. Thereafter, India remained a large participant in the trade, but as an exporter of raw cotton, and an importer of finished fabrics. Its own value adding manufacturing sector in between the two ends of trade was squeezed out. With this shift, incomes reduced in India, while investors in industry and trade in Britain became very wealthy. Beckert explains how British merchants persuaded the British government to create regulations governing trade—and even for the management of cotton farming in India—that suited British industry.

In chapters titled, *The Wages of War Capitalism; Capturing Labor, Conquering Land;* and *Slavery Takes Command,* Beckert explains with facts and figures how the ownership of, and trade in, slaves changed the pattern of global trade, making US cotton producers the largest suppliers by displacing Indian farmers, and also made British merchants very wealthy.

In a later chapter, *The New Cotton Imperialism*, he explains how large US retail corporations subsequently took over the power to control global supply chains and fixation of standards and prices around the world.

Beckert's analysis looks at global trade through a broader lens than conventional trade experts do, who focus on volumes, tariffs, and prices. He reveals the sources of political power that cause shifts in trade patterns, as well as the shifts in political power that accompany changing trade patterns. His account of how small, independent farmers and village producers of textiles in India lost their sources of livelihoods, as well as their political power, provides insights into larger, and deeper forces that should be seen by advocates of free trade and global supply chains who, in their pursuit of more globality and large volumes of trade, lose sight of who the winners and losers are, and what they gain and lose beyond incomes.

From a long and wide history of global trade, Beckert provides insights into its effects on local systems. Let me sneak in another recommendation. James C. Scott's seminal account, *Weapons of the Weak: Everyday Forms of Peasant Resistance*, gives deeper, local, insights into the social and political changes that corporatization of agriculture, along with the opening of agriculture markets, can cause. Scott studied the impacts of the 'green revolution' in Malaysia in the 1970s, while the green revolution was underway in Northern India too. Insights specific to Malaysia will not apply to India. However, both Scott's and Beckert's books are worth reading now when Indian farmers are fearing the imposition of free markets and the power of capitalist corporations into their traditional worlds. They provide evidence of social realities that makers of policies must consider, which graphs of incomes and prices and the sizes and productivity of farms cannot.

Building Communities; Local Solutions

The Web of Freedom: J.C.Kumurappa and Gandhi's Struggle for Economic Justice, by Venu Madhav Govindu and Deepak Malghan (academics with the Indian Institute of Science and the Indian Institute of Management in Bangalore), is an eye-opener on the structures of economic systems operating in India. J.C. Kumurappa was sometimes referred to as Gandhi's 'planning commission'. Gandhi's ideas about village communities are generally considered a romantic vision. Govindu and Malghan present Kumurappa's analysis of why local systems solutions developed and implemented by local communities are the only practical way to make systemic changes for inclusive and environmentally sustainable growth.

Kumurappa studied financial accounting in England and public finance in Columbia University. He set up the Davar's College of Commerce in Mumbai with Sorab Davar in the 1920s. It was one of India's earliest schools of 'business management', long before the first Indian institutes of Management were founded in the 1960s.

Kumurappa gave up his accountancy practice and his partnership with Davar, at Gandhi's behest to take up the larger national cause of developing economic solutions for India. He lived among people in rural India for the rest of his life. He listened to them and studied the economics of India, while also developing policies for the Congress party and representing the party in national economic commissions. Like Gandhi, he was also a man of action. He set up the national village industries movement and cooperatives to improve incomes in rural India. (Tragically, the Indian economy is suffering now from policymakers' neglect of village industries and cooperatives which Kumurappa and Gandhi had advocated).

In the chapter titled *India Adrift* the authors record how Kumurappa and Gandhi's strategy for bottom-up development of India's economy was rejected by Jawaharlal Nehru's government which adopted, instead, a strategy of developing the economy top-down from the 'commanding heights', with big factories, big dams, and large organizations. Kumurappa pointed out that both, the Soviet model as well as the Western capitalist model, were top-down models in which the means of production are owned by people at the top—in one case capitalists and in the other bureaucrats. Workers have little room for exercising enterprise in both systems. Moreover, they remain wage workers: the wealth created by their work accumulates elsewhere. Whereas in Gandhi's and his model, the workers would be the owners of their own enterprises and wealth creators for themselves.

Sadly, "Kumurappa has suffered from neglect both during his lifetime and for many decades since, primarily due to the dominance of the ideologies he had vehemently opposed. Mainstream economists can scarcely countenance an upstart who sought to inject moral arguments into economic thought," Govindu and Malghan say.

Economics, experts, and ethics

Michael Sandel, professor of political philosophy and government theory at Harvard University, makes compelling arguments for introducing ethics into the governance of economies. His latest book, *The Tyranny of Merit: What's Become of the Common Good* is the third book I recommend. (Sandel's earlier books, *What Money Can't Buy: The Moral Limits of Markets* and *Justice: What's the Right Thing to Do?* have been bestsellers too.)

Sandel explains in his latest book why there is a justifiable reaction against educated elites and experts around the world, leading to the rise of popular, illiberal and conservative, governments. (Narendra Modi, India's Prime Minister, said, "India needs less Harvard and more hard work.")

Sandel takes apart the liberal idea that every person is a master of her own fate, and that if she is not successful it must be due to some weakness in her. The myth in liberal societies, particularly in the US, is that everyone has an equal opportunity to get an education, to become an entrepreneur, and to become wealthy. Therefore, a person's lack of education and poverty are seen as shortcomings in the person, not flaws in the economic system.

This simplistic view does not see how a person's freedoms are constrained by social and economic structures. Like a bird in an invisible cage, the person has some room to move, but soon hits those invisible walls, and must struggle very hard to break through them. Social and economic systems create such invisible walls, like those for black people in the US, and for Dalits in India. Presuming that everyone has equal freedoms in the economy, economists can prove with their numbers, which show that more black people and Dalits are poor, that they are inherently inferior to others and get what they deserve. The exceptions who do break out are used to prove that if some can do it, everyone can. Therefore, once again, the fault lies with those who do not succeed.

Education systems are more accessible to the elites in the US and are becoming even more so Sandel points out. Those who pass out of the best schools believe they are more meritorious, and therefore their opinions should matter more than of those of the other people who did not get to the top. They look down on 'less qualified' citizens. This is the tyranny of a false merit which, Sandel says, is exacerbating social and political divisions. 'People like us' are not listening to 'people like them'.

The WEIRDest People in the World: How the West Became Psychologically Peculiar and Particularly Prosperous is a recent book by Joseph Heinrich, professor of human evolutionary biology at Harvard University. (WEIRD is Western, educated, industrial, rich, and democratic.) Heinrich supplements Sandel's arguments. He explains how the elite in the West have acquired their beliefs in the essentiality of individual agency and their denigration of traditional norms of social solidarity.

Ethics in science and technology

The 'scientific' Enlightenment arose in Europe in the seventeenth century. From where it has spread around the world, along with Western arms, and Western technologies with the expansion of global trade, as Beckert explains in *The Empire of Cotton*.

Technology has given men great power over other people, and Man great power over Nature. It has created a hubris that, with science and technology, Man can overcome all obstacles to economic progress, including the damage to the natural environment that economic growth with technologies has caused. However, technology has run far ahead of wisdom. It does not understand that all men are sustained by the society around them, and that Man is a part of a large, complex system. Any harm caused to others, and any harm done to Nature by economic growth and technology, harms Man himself.

His Holiness the Dalai Lama calls for a revival of this Eastern wisdom, in *The Universe in a Single Atom: The Convergence of Science and Spirituality*, an analysis of the progress of science and technology. This was the fourth book that Anil let me add to my quota of three.

The Dalai Lama, a keen life-long learner, has been discussing matters of science and spirituality with eminent scientists in the West for decades. Many scientists have also travelled to his home in Dharamshala.

In the conclusion of his book, he writes:

"Scientific knowledge, as it stands today, is not complete. Recognizing this fact, and clearly recognizing the limits of scientific knowledge, I believe is essential.... A full human understanding must not only offer a coherent account of reality, our means of apprehending it, and the place of consciousness but also include a clear awareness of how we should act.... How we view ourselves and the world around us cannot help but affect our attitudes and our relations with our fellow human beings and the world we live in. This in essence is a question of ethics."

My conclusion is, our collective resolution for the New Year must be to recouple the economy with humanity, and technology with ethics.

(Published by Founding Fuel in January 2021)

2

A New Architecture for Global Governance

Economies everywhere have been severely shaken by Covid19. The only 'vaccine' that medical experts could prescribe, until a vaccine safe for humans is developed, was enforced physical separation of people to prevent the virus spreading. Meanwhile, extensive trials of vaccines are underway to ensure they will not have harmful side-effects.

Tragically, the side-effects of the untested treatment already prescribed, i.e. lock downs and physical separation, have damaged many systems on which humans depend for their well-being. They revealed the fragility of public health systems of many countries. Supply chains to provide essential supplies, even for medical needs, were broken. Diversion of medical resources for Covid prevented treatment of patients with other ailments. Livelihoods were disrupted when people could not go out to work and business stopped. Many, living on the edge, slipped into starvation.

The damage is not over. Malnutrition of children will stunt their development. Schools have not been able to open properly. The disruption of education may affect the further development of well-off children too. Less well-off people have suffered the most. Inequalities within societies, which were already high, have been exacerbated.

Many pre-existing conditions, that GDP growth numbers did not reveal, required treatment before Covid. Realizing this, the UN's 17 Sustainable Development Goals (SDGs) were adopted in September 2015. They cover a wide range of problems—inequalities in economies, persistent poverty, poor education and health services, as well as an environmental crisis. The goals describe the morbidities that societies and economies were suffering from before Covid struck them. They were too weak to tolerate the shock of the lock-down medicine.

Global institutions created after the Second World War to solve global problems cooperatively, such as the UN that has led the adoption of the SDGs, and WTO which morphed from GATT, have been struggling to keep the world united. When 'globalization' accelerated with larger flows of trade and finance across national borders since the 1990s, these institutions have been unable to keep the world united. The WTO is in limbo. The WHO, required now to coordinate responses to the Covid pandemic, is caught in a crossfire between the US and China. Mismatches between the capabilities of institutions and the global problems they must address in this century have been starkly revealed.

A new way must be found. Economists are searching for a 'new normal'. Paraphrasing Albert Einstein, he said it is madness to try to solve intractable problems with the same approach that has caused them. Clearly 'Covid time' is the time to think why prevalent approaches for problem solving are inappropriate for solving complex global problems.

Humanity is facing two crises at the same time: a governance crisis and an epistemic crisis. The two are intertwined.

An Epistemic Crisis: The Break-Down of 'Systems Thinking'

Before jumping to any solution, one must first understand the problem. The problem policymakers (and experts) have in the 21st century is that there are many problems, and *all must be solved simultaneously*. The problem cannot be simply broken up into easier to solve pieces. Solutions to environmental problems that aggravate problems of livelihoods cannot be good solutions. Or solutions to economic problems that aggravate environmental problems. Solutions to increase GDP which also increase inequity will not help to make the world better for everyone.

Scientific advances since the European Enlightenment have multiplied the numbers of specialists. An abundance of experts now available to solve diverse problems should be a blessing. However, their abundance has become a problem because experts are too narrowly focused on separate pieces of the system: they are *not able to comprehend the whole system*. Specialists in diseases of the heart do not understand sufficiently the effects of their interventions on other systems in the human body, and patients must turn to other specialists for treatment of the side-effects of the solution to their heart problems. Often, they end up with a mental health specialist to help them manage their confusion and depression, and their anxiety about the cumulative cost of their wonderful treatments.

The economy, society and ecology are integrated in a system. Changes in any one of these components will affect the others. Components of systems must be in harmony with each other for the system to remain healthy. Lock-downs to prevent Covid are an example of unintended consequences of a good solution which were not foreseen because the whole system was not kept in view. Two examples from India also illustrate the harms that can be caused to systems by policies designed by specialists.

Clean air

An unintended benefit of the economy's wheels grinding to a halt, with the severe lockdown imposed in India, was that Delhi's residents saw clear blue skies in the day and stars at night which they had not seen for years. The severe air pollution Delhi has been experiencing in the last decade is an example of good policies combining to produce bad effects. Ever since mechanization was introduced in the 1980s to improve farm productivity, farmers in Punjab have burned the paddy stubble the machines leave. Later, alarmed by the impact thirsty paddy growth was having on dwindling ground water resources, the government passed the Preservation of Subsoil Water Act in 2009. It stipulated that farmers postpone by one month the sowing and transplanting of paddy so that it was closer to the onset of the monsoon. This reduced the need for drawing water from underground for the transplanted paddy.

However, the burning of the stubble post-harvest also got postponed by one month. It now coincided with the onset of winter in the North when wind movement is low and atmospheric moisture content is also high. Thus, two good things together: the improvement of productivity of agriculture with mechanization, and management of water resources, has produced the unintended consequence of Delhi becoming the most polluted city in the world! Sadly, as the wheels of the economy have begun to turn again, pollution is back in Delhi's air. The old normal may be returning.

Education of girls

The other example is from rural Rajasthan. Education of girls gives many benefits to society. Retention of girls in schools in Rajasthan's poorer, water scarce districts has increased in the last ten years with concerted efforts by the government and NGOs to improve education. Also, water conservation programs reduced distances women have to carry water to their homes, thus pressures for adolescent girls to stay home to help their mothers reduced. Two good things together—better education and better water management—produced the desired outcome. However, it is noticed in the last two years that girls have begun to drop out of secondary school. Investigations reveal that the addition of another good program, Swatchh Bharat, to provide toilets in homes was the cause. The toilets required more water to be brought home, and so mothers needed their daughters at home again.

A property of complex systems is that many good things interacting with each together may unwittingly produce bad outcomes. The epistemic problem is, experts mentally break complex systems into parts and then try to improve them separately. Thus, economists worry about the economy, and sociologists about society, and ecologists about ecology. And they quarrel with each other. Economists think ecologists are coming in the way of growth. Sociologists say economists do not understand that humans are human beings and not commodities in labour markets.

In the prevalent paradigm of managing complex systems in governments and large corporations, each part of a complex system is managed by specialists reporting up to the top. There, they try to coordinate the whole system. All have their programmes and their budgets and each passes down instructions to its subordinates in the localities who are responsible for only a part of the system.

A Crisis in Governance: Experts Taking Power Away From the People

Recovery from COVID-19 is an opportunity to create economies that are more resilient and fair. Two architectural principles must apply.

The first principle is, economies of "scale" should be replaced by economies of "scope". A complex global economy in which local producers obtain scale (and lower costs) by supplying products for global markets is vulnerable to shutdowns anywhere. Local economies that have a variety of capabilities within them, albeit on smaller scales, are more resilient. Therefore, local economic webs must be strengthened, in preference to global supply-chains.

COVID-19 has settled, for now, the debate between free-trade evangelists and advocates of industrial policy. The "Make in India" program of the Indian government, which was dismissed by free trade economists as a reversion to protectionism, has become a necessity — to maintain supplies of essentials and to create employment for the hundreds of millions of Indians with fragile incomes who have been badly shaken by the lockdown of the Indian economy.

The second principle is, local systems solutions are essential for global systemic problems. Garrett Hardin had coined the expression, "The Tragedy of the Commons", in 1968, for the proposition that a resource that belongs to everybody will not be cared for by anybody. This supported policies to privatise public property, ostensibly for the benefit of everybody and became the dominant school of economics from the 1970s onwards. "Capitalists" often cite Hardin in their quarrel with "socialists".

Elinor Ostrom, who was awarded the Nobel Prize for economics in 2008 (the first woman economics laureate, after 62 men), offered a different explanation for the tragedy of the commons. She argued that common resources are well-managed when those who benefit from such resources the most are in close proximity to them. For her, the tragedy occurred when external groups exerted their power (politically, economically or socially) to gain a personal advantage. She was greatly supportive of the "bottom-up" approach to issues: Government intervention could not be effective unless supported by individuals and communities, she asserted.

The 'New Normal'

The economics profession rules the shaping of public policies around the world. Since the financial crisis in 2008, which economists could not predict, and which was evidence that their models were incomplete, they been searching for a 'new normal' for the global economy. After Covid it is clear that, even if they could find a new model to sustain economic growth, their model would be incomplete.

Hardin's 'Tragedy of the Commons' leads to the conclusion that human beings are incapable of managing something which does not belong to them personally. It is an extension of the belief that humans are purely rational and self-interested actors. Whereas it has been known to poets and politicians for ages that humans have passions and emotions too. Moreover, what the world needs now is humans who care about their global commons.

Economists explain that welfare is produced for everyone by 'an invisible hand' even when everyone is purely self-interested. Ostrom made visible some principles by which the invisible hand works. The rules by which humans agree to govern their affairs, and the powers they assign to institutions to implement the rules on their behalf, are systems of governance created by humans. Institutions of electoral democracy and concepts of limited liability corporations are creations of the human imagination made concrete. Now institutions must change rapidly now to improve the health of societies, economies, and the environment, to achieve the SDGs.

Changes must be made in the design of business institutions: their purpose must not be purely the business of making profits for investors; they must also account for their impacts on the environment and social conditions.

'Government of the people, for the people, and *by* people' is the essence of democratic governance. However, even where there is constitutional democracy with equal voting rights for everyone, rich and poor, men and women, and whatever their religion, as India has, governance is not *by* the people. People are managed by experts, who are supposed to know what is best for the people, and who must apply their expert knowledge to find solutions for the people. This is the common approach, whether the government is a totalitarian one as the Soviet Union was, or a democratic one like the US where the President's councils of expert advisers design policies.

As explained before, this is the wrong approach for solving complex problems which manifest in different shapes in different places. For example, environmental problems combine with livelihood problems in different ways in the Himalayan mountains in the North of India, in the dry lands of Rajasthan in the middle, and in the lush coastal regions of Kerala in the South.

Therefore, *local systems solutions are necessary for such global systemic problems*. The solution is, responsibility for the governance of complex systems must be devolved to communities in their localities. However, not only politicians, also experts at the top, are reluctant to let go of their power. They claim that the locals will not have the capability to manage, and so the centre must take on the burden of managing the locals.

Redesigning the architecture of global governance institutions

Resentment of elitist experts who look down on them as they govern them is a reason for the rise of populist movements in many countries. It caused Brexit in Britain and the election of Donald Trump in the US. In India, Prime Minister Modi declared, 'We need hard work, not Harvard'.

The Indian Constitution requires power to be devolved to elected bodies in towns and villages. It has not happened in practice even in seventy years since the Constitution was adopted in January 1950. India's economy has been growing quite well since the 1990s, after India joined the global economy which was also growing well. For many years India's economy was the fastest growing large economy following China's. However, India's track record of improvement of social and environmental indicators has not been good. For India to achieve the SDGs, India's approach to governance must change. Solutions must be found and implemented by communities, and not by experts in Delhi or in the state capitals.

India changed the charter and name of its central planning institution in 2014. The old Planning Commission was replaced by the National Institution for Transforming India (NITI Aayog). The top-down budget controlling powers of the Planning Commission were withdrawn. NITI was chartered to build capacities for governance in the states and in local bodies, and to promote cooperative federalism.

Names are easy to change, behaviours more difficult, and it is never easy to give up power. It has taken a while for transformations in NITI to show up. Its innovative 'Aspirational Districts Program' (ADP) gives great hope. Two years ago, NITI focussed on 112 of the country's 640 districts. These are the furthest behind in terms of the SDGs, and economically poorest too. Partnerships were formed in each district between local government functionaries, NGOs, and corporate philanthropies. The districts were provided score-cards of where they stood with respect to conditions that mattered to the people—health and nutrition, education, agriculture and water resources, financial inclusion and skill development, and basic infrastructure. NITI is playing the role of cheer-leader and score keeper, and also provides a platform for sharing lessons learned.

An evaluation of progress so far by independent Indian and US think tanks has shown the efficacy of this approach of partnerships on the ground to solve complex systemic problems. The aspirational districts are improving much faster all round than they were with the previous top-down expert driven approach. The reasons for some amongst them improving even faster than others are found to be: the facilitative role played by the local government leaders; and the willingness of experts from the philanthropies to trust the people to find the best solutions rather than forcing best practices from elsewhere onto them.

This turns on its head the belief that when problems are large and global they need an expert-driven, central organization to solve them 'on scale'. Governance within countries must devolve further down, not move up, to solve complex problems. And freedoms to govern must move down to countries from international bodies.

The role of central bodies within countries, and internationally too, must be to help locals build their own capacities for solving their problems. Central bodies can convene the locals to share learnings, and to deliberate on rules for governing their collective commons. They must resist the temptations of power—both political power as well as expert power.

The G-20 is in a special place amongst global institutions. It does not have a long history: it is young. It does not yet have a rigid structure nor a large body. It can shape itself to be a catalyst of change in global governance—even guiding changes in other global institutions like the WTO, the UN, and the Security Council. Because, as Einstein said, humanity will not be able to find a new, harmonious and sustainable normal with old mind-sets of governance.

(Published by the Global Solutions Journal in January 2021)

3

The Software of Democracy

Democracy is in peril: forms of electoral democracy that conventional democrats rely on are clearly strained.

Vaclav Havel, the Czech stateman and writer, who served as the first President of Czechoslovakia in 1989 when the Soviet Union collapsed, and then as the first President of the Czech Republic until 2003, had become disillusioned with political parties and the venality of democracy's political institutions. In 2000, he formed "Forum 2000", an annual convention of democratic thinkers from around the world in Prague to discuss the strengthening of people's democracy. I have participated in the Forum's lively meetings in Prague. Forum leaders worried about the rising tide of anti-democratic authoritarianism (within electoral democracies) in neighbouring Poland and Hungary, and within the Czech Republic too, as well as in Italy and France. Over many tankards of good Czech beer, I debated with university students, in the same café in which Havel and his friends had plotted the demise of Soviet hegemony in Czechoslovakia. The evangelism in the earlier meetings of the Forum, of spreading European Enlightenment to the rest of the world, was subdued by fear of the return of darkness in their own lands. By 2016, the shadow of democracy's decline had even extended across the Atlantic to the USA, the shining beacon of democratic liberty.

The Czech honeymoon with electoral democracy lasted less than two decades. The global fling with social media, with the expectation that it could circumvent political institutions, and bring all citizens together, has lasted even less. Friendster, the first social network went live in 2002. Linked-In, Facebook, YouTube, and Twitter followed within five years. Social media has failed to reduce social distancing. Instead it has widened divisions within electoral democracies. More dangerously, it has surfaced and aggravated social disharmony. Now democratically elected governments are struggling to rein in privately controlled social media which is corrupting electoral processes and corroding social harmony.

Rebuilding the Democratic Enterprise

Institutions—of the state, of business, of democracy, of justice—have been developed over centuries by human beings to fulfil the needs of their societies. Institutions are the vehicles with which societies realise their aspirations. Indeed, Homo sapiens can be distinguished from other animal species by its *deliberate* development of institutions for the management of its affairs. Animal, bird and insect communities have innate, institutionalised rules that govern their behaviour. But so far as we know they do not, unlike human beings, consciously change and improve these institutionalised rules.

Douglass C. North received the Nobel Prize in economics in 1993 for his work on the development of institutions and their role in human progress. North defined institutions as 'the humanly devised constraints that structure political, economic and social interactions'. Constraints, he said, are devised as formal rules (constitutions, laws, property rights) and informal restraints (sanctions, taboos, traditions, codes of conduct).

Institutions create a house within which human beings can live with each other. A house needs structures and systems to function. It needs walls to divide space into rooms. And it needs systems for ventilation, electric supply, and plumbing. However, structures and systems do not by themselves make a house into a functioning home for its occupants. A happy home is made by the practices and habits of those who live in it. Therefore it should not be surprising that a happy, functioning family and an unhappy, dysfunctional family could be living in identical houses: because while they may live within identical structures, the pattern and quality of their interactions could be very different

No doubt the architecture of the house can influence the pattern of interaction of its residents. Though all houses may have some common rooms, such as a living room in which people could come together, one house could have many private rooms which people can maintain according to their own tastes, whereas another could have fewer, larger rooms that require people to negotiate the use of those rooms with each other. But, whatever be the arrangement of the walls and rooms, it is the respect people have for each other and the quality of their interactions that distinguish happy homes from unhappy ones.

Like a house, democracy requires structures and systems for it to function. And like a home, it also needs institutionalized practices for people to live together happily. Structures in democracy delineate the roles of the legislature, the judiciary, and the executive. They also divide authorities and responsibilities amongst the centre, the states, and local bodies. The number of political parties is another dimension of structure.

The principle of majority rule—that the will of the majority, determined by voting, should prevail—is a central tenet in democracies. However, a problem with this principle is that minorities can be unreasonably subjugated, even tyrannized, by laws 'democratically' framed by the majority. An egregious example is Adolf Hitler and the Nazi Party in Germany. Elected by a majority of German citizens, Hitler and the Nazis viciously persecuted a minority—the Jewish citizens. Examples such as these suggest that elections and votes should not be the only or even the principal operative structures on which democracy depends. Democracies must have other structures and processes to include all people and ensure they are justly treated. Law courts are one such structure. But courts are enjoined to interpret and apply laws, and not create their own laws. Since the laws are created by the principle of majority rule, the judiciary cannot be a remedy for the structural limitation of a democracy that is overly dependent on this principle.

Examining structures of democracies in thirty-six countries, Arend Lijphart analyses two basic patterns of democracies in his book, *Patterns of Democracy: Government Forms and Performance in Thirty-Six Countries* (Yale University Press, 1999). One is 'majoritarian' and the other is 'consensual'. In majoritarian democracies, majority rule is the norm. (Generally there are two principal parties in such democracies, but there could be more). The party that gets the most votes rules and the power to govern is then concentrated in this party. The losers must oppose. The tyranny of the majority is expected to be mitigated by the rotation of the party in power over time. On the other hand, in consensual democracies power is spread across more organs of the state and perhaps amongst more political parties also. Britain, according to Lijphart is the most majoritarian of the thirty-six democracies he has studied and Switzerland the most consensual.

One would expect that consensual democracies, as analysed by Lijphart, where power is more devolved and there are more political parties would be slower to arrive at agreements and hence less efficient. For example, Switzerland has three official languages and is divided into many independent cantons. The Swiss must work harder to ensure that solutions work for all than people in democracies like Britain which is united by one language and has much less devolution of powers. Therefore Lipjhart's analysis that consensual democracies generally perform better than majoritarian democracies is surprising.

There may be two explanations for this. One is that the measures of performance Lipjhart uses include many social measures, such as health, education, crime, care of the elderly, and care of the environment, in addition to economic growth. Consensual democracies have 'kinder, gentler, qualities', he says. The other explanation could be that majoritarian democracies breed dissent: losers make it their business to make life difficult for the winners. With weaker processes for arriving at consensus, differences are more difficult to resolve in majoritarian democracies. Thus decision-making stalls when collaboration is required between the governing party and the opposition. Reforms in the US have been stymied for many years by stand-offs between the two opposing parties.

The Hardware and Software of Democracy

The formal institutions of an electoral democracy are 'vertical' institutions, for upward elections of representatives of the people below, into Parliaments and Congresses, and for the election of a supreme executive leader in Presidential democracies. The powers of these elected leaders above are expected to be constrained by other institutions on top—principally, independent courts of justice, as well as other independent bodies such as election commissions. These are the hardwired structures of a democratic system. The informal institutions of democracies which connect citizens laterally, in communities of interest, and the informally coded rules of conduct amongst themselves, are the software of democracy.

In a discussion in New York in 2004 about the condition of democracy in the world, in which I participated, a woman from California bemoaned the deterioration of democracy in her state into a series of direct ballots on various issues, each explained either in thick documents that nobody had time to read or in contentious, partisan, media debates that illuminated nothing more than the hate the opposing parties had for each other. She said that it was a fallacy to think that voters who had been to university (she herself had a PhD) were 'educated' about the issues they were expected to vote on. The processes of public debate were failing to educate the people about these issues and hence all votes, even of the so-called educated elite, were merely an expression of their personal prejudices. In that way California, she said, was no different to India in that people, whether educated or not, voted according to their identities and their prejudices. She said that dialogic processes are essential to prevent democracy deteriorating into a mechanical charade of efficient balloting and counting of votes.

With this analysis, some assertions may now be made about the structures and processes required for a healthy democracy. A popular view of democracy—that it is principally a system of fair (and frequent) elections to determine the will of the majority—which is projected in TV pictures of people lining up at polling booths in Afghanistan, Iraq, and other such newly 'democratized' countries in US-led campaigns to spread democracy through the world, is a dangerously facile view. The essence of democracy is people's participation in deliberations, in many forums, to democratically determine policies that affect their lives. This leads to the conclusion that the quality of their deliberations and their respect for others' views, and not the fairness of elections may be the key to effective democracy.

The design of democracy's structures—constitutions, devolved institutions, and electoral processes—is important for democracy to function smoothly.

However, the nature of the dialogue and deliberations of citizens within (and outside) these structures produces democracy's quality. The structures are like the walls and doors and systems of the house. Or like the hardware of a computer. Whereas dialogue and deliberations are the software of democracy. And, as in computer systems, given adequate hardware, the system's performance depends entirely on the quality of the software.

Democracy in Reality on the Ground

A Government *of* the people—*(could be a good, authoritarian government that imposes laws)*, as well as a Government *for* the people—*(a benign authoritarian government)* maybe good definitions of good governance. But, they are not descriptions of good *democratic* governance. Good democratic governance must be *by* the people also.

Good, democratic, citizens take care of the society around them and the 'commons' around them too, and not just concern themselves with their individual interests. Thus, the liberal enterprise, focussed excessively on the rights of individuals, is at odds with the democratic enterprise, which insists that citizens take responsibility for the conditions of others around them, as well as the conditions of society and Nature that nurtures them.

As an aside, this is the fundamental weakness in concepts of responsibilities of capitalist firms. They are given all rights of citizens in society—the rights to property, the rights to free speech, the rights to due process of law, the rights to sue others, but their responsibilities are to produce results only for their investors and owners. Thus, capitalist corporations are, by legal design, selfish citizens of societies. They are not required by law or by societal conventions to be 'trustees' of the community's resources—human as well as environmental--that they use in their operations. Therefore, the design of the corporate business institution, which is the principal engine of capitalist economic growth, must be changed for capitalism to become more democratic.

Gandhiji said India will not become a democratic country where citizens have all freedoms—political, social, and economic—unless there is democracy in the villages. The 'software' of democracy is essential for citizens in local communities to live democratically and harmoniously together. They would require some 'hardware' also, such as locally elected bodies for governing their local affairs. These local bodies must be accountable for matters that are best managed locally, such as the interplay of local environment resources and economic activities, and equal access to public services for all local citizens regardless of caste, religion, and economic circumstances.

Responsibilities for solving complex problems, in which many systems interact, such as the environment system, the social system, and the economic system, must be handed downwards because such problems take different shapes in different situations. One size solutions cannot fit all. Therefore, the solution usually adopted for solving complex problems, which is to kick them up to experts (who usually operate in their silos of expertise), cannot work. *Local systems solutions, devised and implemented collaboratively by stakeholders in local communities, is the scientific solution to global systemic problems the world is facing, which are enumerated in the SDGs.* It is also the fundamental fix for democracy.

Three Layers of Institutions

The problem with a majoritarian democracy is that it is not designed to find solutions for complex problems with many points of view. A government with a majority, especially a large one, can become as authoritarian as a dictatorial one. It can deny minorities their rights for their views to be considered while framing laws and resolving contentious issues. The people have spoken once in the election; that should be enough. Now, they must leave it to the government in power. Thus, a government elected by a majority can justify the exclusion of the minority. However, by excluding the views of the many that did not vote for it — and quite often these may even be the majority in the first-past-the-post system — a government reduces its own effectiveness.

When problems are complex, good governance requires effective methods for people's participation. Referendums of the entire electorate give an illusion of good democracy — that the people have been consulted. Politicians on both sides of a referendum will run populist campaigns appealing to the basest of instincts to sway the opinions of the masses. Whereas, when the issue is complex, voters should be educated about what they are voting for. And then, when a small majority determines how all must go (52% wanted Britain to leave the European Union versus 48% that did not), referendums become yet another example of the problem with a majoritarian democracy rather than a good solution.

Healthy democracies need three vibrant layers of institutions. At the bottom is the public space and the media in which people must be free to speak up if they want to. On the top is the layer of constitutional institutions — parliaments, courts, etc. Social media has enlarged the public space enormously. Many more people are speaking up and many issues are being raised. Social media provides a good platform for opposing views, but is glaringly inept at reconciling them. On the contrary it is heightening divisive walls. Therefore, more problems require the attention of constitutional institutions above, and they have more on their plate than they can digest.

When elected representatives are expected to vote in their assemblies only according to the wishes of their own constituency and to also follow party whips, they cannot open their minds to listen to the views of other constituents. Thus, assemblies of elected representatives, in which framers of the U.S. Constitution hoped representatives would deliberate upon what is best for the whole system and not just for their parts of it, have become incapable of performing the role they should perform.

With democratic governance slipping into ineffectual log-jams, it is tempting to close down the public space at the bottom, or to impose a majoritarian view from above to strengthen the government. There is fear that India may be slipping down this path, which may strengthen government on the ground, while stifling democratic governance. It is the road to 'maximum government, minimum governance'.

Political middles are thinning in democracies everywhere. People want change. Radical parties of the Right and Left are gaining support. The solution for strengthening governance and democracy at the same time is to strengthen the middle layer of institutions within democracies that lie between the open public sphere and formal government institutions. These are spaces where citizens with diverse views can listen to each other, and understand the whole system of which they are only parts. Neither elected assemblies nor social media provide such spaces. Sadly, even think tanks have become divided along ideological and partisan lines.

It is imperative for India to build intermediate level, unofficial or semi-official institutions for non-partisan deliberation amongst concerned citizens. Democratically inclined governments should encourage such institutions to form and operate. However, as we will discuss later, democratically elected authoritarian governments are unlikely to officially provide them more space.

Change from Within

Human societies are complex, multi-faceted, and 'self-organizing' systems. Their impetus to re-organize themselves arises from within themselves. Even when a society is colonised by another people who want to impose their ideas and their model of organization onto them, colonised societies will resist. Therefore, wise rulers allow local ideas to help shape new systems so that they can be well-rooted and sustainable.

Established paradigms are hard to change as Thomas Kuhn explained in his seminal treatise, *The Structures of Scientific Revolutions*. The beneficiaries of an established paradigm, even in the physical sciences, resist change. Their benefits from it are their status in society, the power they derive from their status, and often are pecuniary too. The instinct of self-preservation will make them fight hard to deny any evidence that challenges their supremacy. Kuhn was describing ideas in the physical sciences, such as the position of the earth in the solar system, where new evidence is harder to deny than in the social and economic sciences where data is perforce more fuzzy. Changing paradigms of governance in social and economic spheres, where data is less 'hard', and where emotions and perceptions matter, is more difficult.

Changes in established governance systems are unlikely to come from within those who are in institutions of power. In fact, they are expected to defend the established institutions to provide society with stability: presidents, supreme court judges, and members of Parliament must swear to defend their countries' constitution as it is. Therefore the pressure to change must come from outside these hard-wired institutions. Even then the established institutions will resist being changed. Therefore, forces outside the established institutions must be strategic and better organized in movements for change to have an effect on an established way of governance. History reveals that it is always "the people"—i.e. civil society—who have compelled fundamental change in systems of governance. Therefore, we should not be surprised that governments who are worried about their loss of power with change will be wary of civil society movements. Asking established governments to give a greater role to civil society is unlikely to be a good strategy for change. Therefore, civil society actors must develop strategies for change based on an understanding of their own place within democracy's structures.

The open public space raises concerns. These are many and not easy to reconcile. Social media has greatly increased the noise in the public space. Which are the signals from the noise that the formal institutions of governance should respond to?

The layer of civil society above the open public space provides the intermediate layer for democratic deliberation amongst citizens. This is where citizens can listen to each other, and together develop broad contours of solutions that will not harm anybody. This 'pre-digestion' is essential to enable the formal institutions of democracy above to function in the interests of all the people. Democracies are having indigestion because this vital, intermediate layer has not grown to cope with the pressure of demands and conflicts from below. In fact, it is diminishing.

Political paradigms are changed by revolutions: some violent; others non-violent. All change, revolutionary or evolutionary, is propelled by ideas. Thoughtful citizens, who care for the condition of their societies, must rebuild the intermediate 'glue' between the noisy, open public space and the rigidities of formal institutions. They can do this by being an example of open-minded dialogue amongst citizens with different histories and different perspectives of reality.

Some tips from Gandhiji for those who want to be seeds of a snowball of a large movement of change.

- Be the change you want to see in the world.
- Don't be in haste to act until you have understood.
- Open the windows of your own mind to let many ideas flow into it.
- Hear many voices. Learn from them.

In a world too easily divided into people we are against and people we are with, beware that your ideas, no matter how scientifically right they may seem to you to be, may be dismissed by others because of "whose side" you are seen to be on. Therefore, before you speak, and while you form your ideas, ensure that the "we" of who you are, not only includes many points of view, but is also seen to include many points of view.

Let us not be in haste to make any 'concrete' recommendations to make changes to institutions that must be fixed no doubt, such as the electoral funding system, the police, the judicial system, etc. Many commissions have been charged to do this in the past. They have even placed their recommendations before the government and the Parliament. One that Sam and I are very familiar with is the 2nd Administrative Reforms Commission who consulted with all political parties and all states and produced 15 reports on judicial reforms, police reforms, reforms of bureaucracy, etc. Its recommendations were accepted by government but they are not implemented. It was not even the first official commission on such matters, nor is it the most recent one on some of them. Yet there is no significant change. The recent impasse on agriculture reforms is another instance, where the government cites the number of expert commissions that have recommended reforms in the last twenty years and yet they are not implementable.

The flaw may be in the theory-of-change adopted to bring about change in complex systems with many stakeholders and many perspectives. Expert driven solutions without sufficient participation of stakeholders through the process, for understanding what the issues are, and for developing the contours of solutions, will be resisted by stakeholders, and will be hard to implement.

(Essay written for discussion in a study-circle in January 2021).

4

Effective Coalitions Form Bottom-Up and Not Top-Down

Coalitions are invariably necessary for addressing the complex issues that civil society organisations are motivated to work on. They are required to aggregate adequate resources and bring together diverse capabilities.

Philanthropists and corporations with CSR ambitions, often form coalitions amongst themselves to aggregate financial resources to have 'impact at scale'. Generally, their theory when shaping the coalition is that they should focus on one cause, combine their resources, and push out a common solution as widely as possible—a 'one-size-fits-all' approach.

Other forms of coalitions bring diverse partners together, from across the corporate/philanthropic, civil society, and government sectors. The reason for this is the understanding that complex issues require combinations of diverse perspectives for a good understanding of the challenge, and to provide diverse capabilities for the delivery of the solution.

The former, single stakeholder type of coalition, though limited in its capability, is simpler to set up. Nevertheless, even such coalitions have difficulties in forming and performing. Issues of 'brands', decision rights, and even personal egos, come in the way. Attention to the scale of the outcome in terms of sustainable impact on the lives of people, slips too easily into attention to the scale of the coalition itself, and to impacts on the brands of the partners involved.

Coalitions amongst civil society organisations are bedeviled by similar, self-centered concerns, even when they are focused on a single cause—for example, the rights of women, or the needs of children. Who will be invited to high-level meetings with governments? Who will get the most credit for the outcome? When coalitions aim to be broader, difficulties in forming coalitions increase. For one, the coalition must have a common purpose for its existence and a common goal to align partners' actions. Another, is the requisite architecture for the coalition.

The recent history of the labour rights movement in India provides insights into some of these challenges. Indian labour unions have been struggling for some years to combine their energies to serve the crying needs of marginalised workers, who are in informal employment or in self-employment, have no protections of their rights to speak of, and no social security.

The unions have been unable to form an effective coalition for the common cause of India's workers because they cannot agree amongst themselves on the methods of action to apply, and because they mistrust each other's broader political intentions. They have realised that unions are mistrusted because they are perceived to be serving the interests of their own leaders, and only the small number of workers in the organised sector. They must change public perceptions and win the right to represent all of India's workers. Therefore, many have been working on the ground to provide relief to families in distress, even before the pandemic struck, and they have multiplied their efforts since then.

Some unions believe that the Establishment must be confronted, because sitting around with it in tripartite negotiations has failed to achieve any fundamental changes in the conditions of Indian workers.

These same questions—about appropriate methods and about ultimate objectives—seem to arise in other civil society coalitions also. Putting it bluntly: Is it a matter of only service to the people through relief and development, or also of fighting for their rights?

Formation and Governance of Coalitions

Civil society organisations must become parts of two types of coalitions to produce sustainable all-round change in the lives and livelihoods of people marginalised by the prevalent socio-economic structures.

One is the single stakeholder type—that is a coalition amongst civil society organisations, as mentioned before. The other is coalitions that include other stakeholders too—the institutions who have wealth, governments who have power, and the people as well.

It is important that civil society's leaders build good coalitions at the top for building better multi-stakeholder coalitions on the ground, if we are to achieve future goodness of humanity and the planet.

Civil Society Coalitions

Coalitions of civil society organisations, whose core purpose is to make sustainable improvements in the lives of the poorest citizens of society, and who are also concerned with threats to their existence from the Establishment, may find some common cause with labour unions. They will also be confronted with similar issues in forming effective coalitions. These are:

1. What is the reason for forming a coalition—what is its purpose?

2. Is it a tactical coalition, for a short-term objective? And will we disband when we have achieved it (or failed to achieve it)?

3. Or, are we united for a superordinate purpose, which will provide us a glue to stay together and win the war, with several tactical campaigns on the way?

4. Are we all committed to this superordinate purpose?

5. If we want 'scale' in our coalition so that we can overcome challenges, and we also want the strengths of diverse capabilities, who will we admit into our coalition, and who will we shun?

6. Who is the 'we' that will decide whom to admit?

7. Do we see ourselves as an 'organisation' with conventional structures of governance? Or, will we operate as a network, or even only as a movement?

8. How much structure do we need to define while we are getting going? And, a related question—what would be appropriate structures for providing adequate coherence to shape an energetic movement or an effective network?

Multi-Stakeholder Coalitions

Holistic, sustainable changes on the ground, that benefit *and* empower people, require collaboration between the different sources of power—the power of the people, the power of money, and the power of government authority.

There is little benefit to the people by stakeholders forming coalitions only at the top and declaring goals for change in the world, if their representatives do not collaborate with each other on the ground, and if they do not make improvements in the lives of people, which is their common objective.

The Sustainable Development Goals (SDGs) point to the way to address this challenge. The first 16 SDGs address the many and multi-faceted challenges facing humanity that must be addressed very urgently. None of the SDGs can be addressed without multi-stakeholder collaboration. Moreover, multi-stakeholder teams, working on each of the 16 goals, must work with each other too, because all the goals are systemically interconnected. The 17th SDG—the need for better partnerships—is the key to achieving the other SDGs.

Good coalitions at the top are hard to form because the partners are divided by invisible walls created by competition for recognition, and with jockeying for control. These walls also tend to extend all the way down the rank and file of their organisations.

Convergence Amongst All Stakeholders Must Happen on the Ground

The world needs local systems solutions to solve global systemic problems. Therefore, all civil society actors—other than pure activists perhaps—must be good multi-stakeholder coalition builders on the ground. They must have the ability to facilitate systems thinking and collaborative action on the ground—which must be a common capability for all, irrespective of the specific causes they are committed to.

Effective coalitions form bottom up, not top down. The people on the ground must set the agenda, because they are the common cause that the coalition at the top was formed for.

(Published by the Indian Development Review in July 2020)

5

Who Will Robots and Elephants Vote for: Donald Trump or Xi Jinping?

When the summer holidays come to an end, some magazines ask authors to write about the best books they read in the summer. Though no one has asked me, I want to write what I learned from five books. I found them illuminating because they provided me with answers to three big questions on my mind. First the questions. Then I will tell you about the books.

The three questions are:

1. Can one ever understand complex phenomena through Big Data analytics?

2. Can artificial intelligence (AI) machines replace human beings?

3. Why are rational liberals marooned amidst a sea of 'alternative truths'?

Underlying these questions are two big concerns:

1. Competition between robots and humans for jobs which, many fear, robots are winning.

2. Ideological conflicts, within countries and across national boundaries, are becoming sharper.

The five books are:

1. *How Not to be Wrong: The Power of Mathematical Thinking*, by Jordan Ellenberg

2. *The Social Importance of Self-Esteem*, edited by Andrew M. Mecca, Neil J. Smelser, and John Vasconcellos

3. *Prediction Machines: The Simple Economics of Artificial Intelligence*, by Ajay Aggarwal, Joshua Gans, and Avi Glodfarb

4. *Adi Shankaracharya: Hinduism's Greatest Thinker*, by Pavan K. Verma

5. *The Righteous Mind: Why Good People are Divided by Politics and Religion*, by Jonathan Haidt

These books are an eclectic lot: on mathematics, social sciences, AI technology, moral science, and Hindu philosophy. Together, through their different perspectives, they provided me with insights into the big questions on my mind.

To do justice to them, my essay on what I learned is much longer than the tweets, 'elevator talks', and short blogs that busy people say is all they have time for. To make it easier for my readers, I have divided my essay into three parts.

- In the first part, I write about what I learned about the potential of Big Data and AI—subjects that are very popular now.

- In the second part I go back to insights from the Vedas and wisdom from the past.

- From there, in part three, I come back to the present and suggest a good way to create a more sustainable and harmonious future for our children and grandchildren.

PART 1: DATA, AI AND THE WORLD OF HUMANS

From Mathematics to Economics

Ellenberg's *How Not to be Wrong* is advertised as one of Bill Gates' 10 favourite books. It is an elegant account of the development of mathematical thought over centuries. Applying mathematicians' methods to examples from life around us—election results, sports, biology, and even how the concept of God came about—Ellenberg shows how we can see hidden structures beneath the messy and chaotic structures of our daily lives.

What impressed me most was Ellenberg's analysis of what mathematics cannot explain and why. He says, "Mathematics is a way not to be wrong, but it isn't a way not to be wrong about *everything*. There is a real danger that, by strengthening our abilities to analyse some questions mathematically, we acquire a general confidence in our beliefs, which extends unjustifiably to those things we're still wrong about."

Ellenberg's warning comes to mind while reading the contorted data analyses of some economists in India trying to prove mathematically that the Indian economy has been generating more than enough jobs, in the face of a plethora of anecdotal evidence that Indian youth are under employed and are finding it very difficult to find steady work.

Robert Lucas, who received the Nobel Prize in economics for expounding the 'rational-expectations' view of human behaviour, referred to a theory as something that can be put on a computer and run. The pursuit of numbers, in the belief that numbers alone indicate accuracy, has become the bane of economics. Many forces that shape societies and their economies cannot be easily measured, such as social harmony and citizens' trust in institutions. Such substantial forces must not be excluded from a model which seeks to explain the behaviour of the economy. Economists insist on equations and numbers because that is all that computers can compute, whereas economists should study human behaviour as it is, not as they find easy to model.

In another great book, *Complexity: The Emerging Science at the Edge of Order and Chaos*, which I read 20 summers ago, M. Mitchel Waldorp gives a fascinating account of a meeting in 1987 of economists, including Nobel Laureates Kenneth Arrow and Brian Arthur, with physicists, including Nobel Laureates Murray Gell-Mann and Phil Anderson. The economists wanted to understand what they could learn from physicists about the formulation of theories and models. Economists aspire to model complex socio-economic phenomena in the way physicists model natural phenomena with mathematics. The economists presented their models. Waldorp describes the physicists' reaction:

"And indeed, as the axioms and theorems and proofs marched across the overhead projector screen, the physicists could only be awestruck at their counterparts' mathematical prowess—awestruck and appalled. They had the same objection that Arthur and many other economists had been voicing from within the field for years. 'They were almost too good,' says one young physicist, who remembers shaking his head in disbelief. 'It seemed as though they were dazzling themselves with fancy mathematics, until they really couldn't see the forest for the trees. So much time was being spent on trying to absorb the mathematics that I thought they weren't often looking at what the models were for, and what they did, and whether the underlying assumptions were any good. In a lot of cases, what was required was just some common sense."

The conceptual problem beneath the data scatter diagrams, statistical correlations, and regressions that economists rely on to understand complex phenomena, says Ellenberg, is that these mathematical tools cannot distinguish causation from correlation. Even though two phenomena may be tightly correlated statistically, statistical analysis cannot explain which causes the other, and, indeed, whether there is any causal relationship between them at all. Both of them may arise from a third common cause, from which they both emerge. For example, rich and moist soil will produce more flowers, and more worms too. Observations of numbers of flowers and worms will show both increasing together. Do the worms cause flowers? Or flowers cause worms? One has to look for another cause for both, which could be the condition of the soil.

Adding additional numbers—about the condition of the soil—will show a correlation between all three variables, but it will not explain causal relationships between them. Do more flowers cause the soil to improve, or vice versa? Even if a causal link can be established between two variables, by establishing that one always precedes the other in time, *how* and *why* it causes the other—such as *how* and *why* moist soil induces more flowers—requires a more scientific explanation, with more observations of real things in real places, not merely more data analysis.

Economics is a social science, which economists smitten by mathematics seem to forget. Whereas physicists develop models to predict the behaviour of material particles under the influence of inanimate forces such as gravity and electro-magnetism, economists must predict the behaviours of human beings who have agency, emotions, and aspirations. Humans are not merely 'rational, self-interested' particles, a gross over-simplification which economists make to apply their mathematical equations to predict human behaviour. Moreover, human beings operate within complex environments in which other human beings also have agency, emotions and aspirations. In social analysis, the numbers of interacting variables can become too many to model mathematically.

From Economics to Self-Esteem

The drive to be 'scientific', and by extension quantitative and mathematical, has become very strong in all fields of study. Researchers in social sciences other than economics also find themselves driven to applying mathematics for more 'scientific rigour' to their explanations of human behaviour. They can become even more entangled than economists are, in conceptual confusions that are inherent whenever mathematical approaches are overused to understand complex phenomena, as Ellenberg explains.

'It is the economy, stupid' which makes candidates win elections, former President Bill Clinton said. 'It is self-esteem or lack of it, stupid,' that moves the political base, Donald Trump proved. Hillary Clinton talked about economic policies. Trump talked about making Americans feel great again—particularly blue collar, white workers, who were looked down upon by Clinton (who even described them, disrespectfully as 'white trash'). Trump's policies to revive their jobs—in coal production, and manufacturing—by imposing import duties, and shutting out immigrants have horrified economists. Yet, he was elected President. Similarly, Brexit is strongly supported by Britishers who want to recover control of their own affairs, though it makes no sense to economists.

In India, Prime Minister Narendra Modi may try hard to shift the political discourse towards growth of the economy, and away from societally divisive issues of caste and religion. Ironically, his drive to build pride in an Indian identity has stirred up contentions about 'who' an Indian is, and has caused more divisiveness which is hurting economic growth.

Identity and self-esteem are primal forces that can cause large, social, economic, and even geopolitical problems (like the Western-Muslim cultural conflict). I read *The Social Importance of Self-Esteem*, a scholarly book, to learn more about the connections between self-esteem and societal problems. Neil Smelser says, in the introduction to the book, that some critical questions it explores are (I quote):

- What are the linkages between individual self-esteem and the generation of a social problem?

- How do we measure both of these?

- How do we go about establishing scientifically that connections exist between diminished self-esteem (cause) and the kind of behaviour that constitutes a social problem (effect)?

He points out that what is considered a 'social problem' is determined by cultural values. And that cultural values change. Child labour has become less acceptable in most countries than it used to be. Whereas child-bearing out of wedlock is becoming more acceptable in many. In some societies, even today, child-bearing out of wedlock is considered a social problem whereas child labour is not. While in other societies, child labour is considered a social problem, whereas child-bearing out of wedlock may be considered a solution to a more fundamental social problem of suppressed women's rights!

When a person's social esteem is threatened, primal responses can be either to fight or to flee. Indeed, the drive to fight when self-esteem is threatened can lead to extreme violence, and even to suicidal attacks against the oppressors. The other response, of withdrawal from social interactions, causes psychological illness. Both, violence as well as withdrawal, create further social problems. Thus, the 'cause-and-effect' relationship between self-esteem and social problems goes both ways in wickedly reinforcing loops. It cannot be clear what is the 'root cause': does it lie in social conditions or in the psyches of individuals?

Statistical correlation and mathematical analysis can provide weak explanations, at best, of complex systems' phenomena, such as 'a social problem' and 'self-esteem'. Such phenomena cannot be precisely defined and measured; they change dynamically; and can be both cause and effect of each other.

The conclusion of West German researchers, who had undertaken a scientifically rigorous study of 'major social issues of post-modern Western society', which Smelser cites, summarises the challenges in using customary scientific methods to analyse complex systems' problems. Their conclusion was: "We have been able to determine that we can neither define nor measure either 'social crises' or 'post-modern Western society'. That concludes our report". This is quite an indictment of the over-use of deductive, quantitative methods to understand social phenomena!

From Self-Esteem to Robots

Henry Ford I, the pioneer of mass production, is reported to have complained, 'Why is it every time I ask for a pair of hands, they come with a brain attached?' Human beings have emotions and can feel a loss of self-esteem if they are closely monitored by their supervisors (which Charlie Chaplin highlighted in his movie *Modern Times*). Their feeling of persecution by powerful controllers can push them to band together in labour unions. Thus, unions formed in Ford's factories and he fought bitter battles with them.

The advantage of employing robots in place of human beings is that robots do not have emotions. Or do they? Technologists have developed robotic pets, as well as AI therapists, and even robots that one can have a date with. While such machines seem to be able to physically 'feel' as sensitively as humans do, can they feel emotionally? Could they really 'care' for others as human beings do? Do they have self-esteem? Can they be sensitive to the injured self-esteem of others, including those whose jobs they take away?

Agarwal, Gans, and Golfarb, the authors of *Prediction Machines,* work at the Creative Destruction Lab at the University of Toronto which had, they report, "for the third year in a row, the greatest concentration of AI start-ups of any program on earth'. Eric Bryonjolfson, MIT professor and author of *The Second Machine Age,* endorses their book. He writes, "If you want to clear the fog of AI hype and see clearly the core of AI's challenges and opportunities for society, your first step should be to read this book."

The authors of *Prediction Machines* say, "Our first key insight is that the new wave of artificial intelligence does not actually bring us intelligence but instead a critical component of intelligence—prediction". The question therefore is: So, what else is there to human intelligence that AI does not have? The answer is: 'judgement'. And judgement, the authors suggest, is the ability to choose amongst options to produce the outcome desired. The choice of the outcome desired involves questions of ethics and morality, as we will discuss later. Judgement is required also to give weightage to different options, and to act even when there is insufficient information, which human beings generally do.

Computation makes arithmetic cheap, and so, the authors point out, "Not only do we use more of it for traditional applications of arithmetic, but we also use the new cheap arithmetic for applications not traditionally associated with arithmetic." There is an old joke, that to a consultant with a hammer every problem is a nail. He will use the hammer even when it is not the right tool for the problem. Similarly, there is a temptation now to use powerful computers and Big Data analytics to solve problems that quantitative data and mathematical analysis cannot solve. Ellenberg's warning in *How Not to be Wrong: The Power of Mathematical Thinking* is worth recalling: "There is a real danger that, by strengthening our abilities to analyse some questions mathematically, we acquire a general confidence in our beliefs, which extends unjustifiably to those things we're still wrong about."

AI machines have beaten human masters in chess and even in Go, an even more complex game. This is considered evidence that computers have become more intelligent than human beings. In games like chess and Goh, the aim of the game is clear, and so are the rules of the game. Whereas the aim of a human life is not clear. What is its purpose?

The New York Times article by Cade Metz reports a conversation with a researcher in AIOpen, the AI lab in San Francisco founded by Elon Musk., which raises an intriguing question.

"The (researcher) showed off an autonomous system that taught itself to play Coast Runners, an old boat-racing video game. The winner is the boat with the most points that also crosses the finish line. The result was surprising: the boat was far too interested in the little widgets that popped up on the screen. Catching these widgets meant scoring points. Rather than trying to finish the race, the boat went point-crazy."

AI is enabling machines to do almost everything human beings can do—they beat humans in complex games and they can drive cars through traffic too. Researchers find that, nevertheless, machines need human guidance to tell them what the purpose of the game is. Intelligent machines can go berserk. 'In some ways, what these scientists are doing is a bit like a parent teaching a child right from wrong', says Metz.

Ada Lovelace, who wrote the first program to compute numbers, in the early 1800s, said, "A computer has no pretensions to originate anything. It can do whatever we order it to perform." This has changed with the advent of AI, which is founded on the abilities of computers now to manipulate massive amounts of data, several orders of magnitude greater than what Lovelace had envisaged. With the availability of masses of data for computers to learn from, AI programs have acquired 'deep learning' ability that Lovelace did not foresee. Now, cutting edge AI programs can 'teach themselves'.

While AI programs can teach themselves how to predict more accurately, they cannot teach themselves how to make moral and ethical decisions. Indeed, even when there is no ethical issue involved, but the situation is complex and novel nevertheless and the computer has no prior experience of it, it needs to observe how a human being handles the situation and learn from the human being. Thus, AI programs for self-driving cars observe what a human does when an unusual combination of external conditions as well as malfunctions in the car occurs, and it builds this into its memory to use when and if it encounters a similar situation.

AI programs have huge memories of data they can tap into almost instantaneously, but they do not have the ability to make 'judgements' when there is insufficient data, and especially when ethical issues are involved. Sometimes ethical judgements have to be made while driving a car. If a child suddenly crosses the road should the driver swerve sharply and risk the lives of the passengers in the car? Maybe he should. What if a dog crosses the road? Or a cow? The judgement involves values assigned to the lives of animals, children, and cows. Societal values differ across societies, and they also evolve and change. That is why it is almost impossible, as the authors of *The Social Importance of Self-Esteem* point out, to understand complex social phenomena through statistical correlation and mathematical analysis. Therefore, AI, whose power comes from statistical correlation and mathematical analysis of masses of data, cannot have all the components of intelligence that human beings have.

Henry Ford was concerned that his workers had not only hands to do the work, but human feelings too. Will an AI program managing a factory have any concern for the self-esteem of human workers in the factory? Amazon's enormous fulfilment centres, which are managed with computer programs, are becoming notorious for the pressure they put on workers to perform. Therefore, the rights of workers in the retail industry to represent themselves through labour unions is once again becoming a contentious political issue in the US.

I was amused to see a new book in a bookstore in San Francisco last week. Its title was, *Robot Sex: Social and Ethical Implications!* AI machines have been developed that can serve as pets (in place of living dogs and cats), and one can even have 'a date' with an AI program. It seems one can even have sex with a robot. Could a robot be charged with sexual harassment? The ethical implications of such developments of technology are beginning to worry people. Science can tell us *what is,* and technology enables us *to do.* Technology cannot tell us *what is the right thing to do.* For answers to that perennial question, we must turn to philosophy.

What sort of world will the proliferation of AI and robots create for human beings? What do human beings care about most? These are questions I will turn to in Part 2, which I begin with some eternal questions about human existence that Pawan Verma discusses in his book about Adi Shankaracharya, who he considers Hinduism's greatest thinker.

PART 2: SOCIETAL VALUES AND DOING THE RIGHT THINGS

Who am 'I'?

Adi Shankaracharya, the early 8th century Indian philosopher and theologian, consolidated the doctrine of Advaita Vedanta. He is credited with unifying and establishing the main current thoughts of Hinduism. In *Adi Shankaracharya: Hinduism's Greatest Thinker,* Pawan Verma explains

Shankaracharya's thoughts on the design of the cosmic system and how human beings fit in it.

When did the universe start? What is outside the universe? What was there before it was formed? How did it happen? These are the big questions which the Vedas delved into thousands of years ago, and which Shankaracharya reflected on. Physicists in the 21st century continue to seek answers to these same questions.

Along with these, there are two other questions:

- 'Who' created the universe? The human mind seems to find it hard to conceive that things could happen all by themselves. It instinctively believes that there must be someone 'who did it'. Scientists, on the other hand, search for 'objective' explanations, about causes and effects that are embedded in the design of the system and do not require any 'hidden human hand' to make them work. Thus, there are believers in God (and devotees of different human messengers of God), and there are also atheists who think there is no need for a God.

- Is it possible for a human mind to ever know what is an 'objective' reality? Because, whatever this reality may be outside the human mind, the human mind must know it, and interpret it, through its own 'subjective' construction. It can sense it only through the physical senses it is endowed with, and it has to interpret the information with the programs that operate its own mind's computer.

Shankaracharya was intrigued by the relationships between different phenomena: what is cause and what is effect? He said there were two kinds of interactions between causes and effects. In one, which he called *parinamvada,* the cause changes in order to produce the effect. The second he called *vivartavada,* where the cause itself need not change to produce its effect.

The relationship between the condition of the natural environment and its ability to sustain itself is a *parinamvada* relationship. If the condition of the environment is distorted, it loses its ability to sustain itself. If it does not sustain itself, the condition of the environment will deteriorate further. It is like a chicken-and-egg relationship. When there are more eggs there are likely to be more chickens. And when there are more chickens there are likely to be more eggs. Both, cause and effect change together: because they are the cause of each other. They are *systemically* inter-linked. On the other hand, when a billiards cue hits a billiards ball, the ball's movement is the effect caused by the movement of the cue. However, the condition of the cue is not changed by the movement of the ball. This is an example of a *vivartavada* relationship between a cause and its effect.

The distinction between *parinamvada* and *vivartavada* also explains the existential problem that human beings face. When human beings come to believe that they can be the ultimate movers and shakers of the world, empowered by advances in science and technology, they forget that they are only a part of a larger system that has brought them into existence. They lose sight of the fact that if they change the natural system around themselves, they will be affected by those changes too. Because the sustainability of human existence is dependent on the sustainability of nature.

Zen masters ask their students profound questions ('koans'). By reflecting on these, students may find the ultimate truths of who they are and how they should conduct their lives. One such question is: "Is there a sound in the forest when a big tree falls and there is no one there to hear it?" The insight is: the universe, whatever it is, exists only when the human mind conceives it. Until the human mind thinks about it, who knows, or cares, whether the universe exists!

Albert Einstein said, "Physical concepts are free creations of the human mind, and not, however if may seem, uniquely determined by the external world". (Quoted by Andrew Newberg, Eugene D 'Aquil, and Vincent Raus in *Why God Won't Go Away*, Ballentine Books, 2002). Stephen Hawking wrote, in *A Brief History of Time*, "What we call real is just an idea that we invent to help us describe what we think the universe is like." The insights of the Vedas, Shankaracharya, Einstein, and Hawking all point to the non-existence of a sound in the forest when there is no listener: of the inseparability of subjective perceptions and objective reality.

Zen masters' koans are designed to shake off the struggles of the rational mind; to make it realize the futility of trying to find rational answers to questions that cannot have rational, scientific explanations. When the mind stops thinking rationally, deep insights can alight in it. Shankaracharya calls intuition—the one infallible step which lies beyond reason—*brahmanubhava*. Intuition is the explosive moment when knowledge is instantly transformed into insight.

Verma explains Shankaracharya's legacy in the epilogue of his book. He says there was "an understandable reaction to the uncompromising 'intellectualism' of his vision". And, "there has been a concerted effort to somehow unite the unrelenting non-dualism of Shankaracharya with a theism that is more appealing to ordinary people craving for the grace of a personal god in their search for solace and assurance".

Ramanuja, one of the great minds of Hinduism, who followed Shankaracharya, "was keen to find a way to provide philosophical legitimacy to theism, with all its pageantry of worship and ritual and bhakti", Verma says. Ramanuja understood that Shankaracharya's concepts were, "for lay devotees, much too intellectualized a construct. It did not provide the assurance that human security, need and fulfilment seek in the here and now". Further, most people need "some tangible concept of the absolute to identify with; a divinity that they can internalise in personal terms; the solidarity of faith—not in a concept—but in a deity that is comprehensible".

Hinduism's two great thinkers, Shankaracharya and Ramanuja, were thought-leaders in two different domains of knowledge. One of these domains, primarily Shankaracharya's, may be accessible through the rational, scientific method, and with mathematics and analysis of 'big data'. This is the domain in which 'artificial intelligence' works. The other, primarily Ramanuja's, is beyond the realm of scientific deduction and numbers and mathematics. It becomes accessible through intuition and faith when rationality is suspended.

What is the 'right' thing to do?

Jonathan Haidt's *The Righteous Mind: Why Good People are Divided by Politics and Religion,* is a powerful explanation of the connection (and the competition) between these two realms of knowledge and beliefs. Haidt is a 'cultural psychologist', a discipline that combines an anthropologist's love of context and variability with a psychologist's interest in mental processes. Haidt writes that he obtained some of his deepest insights into the origins of moral ideas during a research project in Odisha in India, where Richard Schweder, whose work had inspired him, had earlier done seminal work in the 1980s.

Living amongst people in Odisha, a state rich in Hindu traditions, with temples and pantheons of gods that people worshiped, Haidt observed two sources of moral codes: one that anthropologists explore, and the other that psychologists' study. Anthropologists study the social and religious traditions through which people learn the societal 'rules of the game' they must observe. Many of these rules, for example those concerning food and sanitation habits (vegetarianism, eating with only the right hand), relations between the sexes (marriage, adultery, etc), relationships amongst members of families (the responsibilities of parents and children for each other), and relationships between people in society more broadly (such as the caste system in Hinduism), are considered moral codes, the breaking of which invites social and religious sanctions. Psychologists and moral philosophers, on the other hand, are interested much more in the inner workings of the human mind.

Haidt uses the lovely metaphor of the elephant and the rider to explain the relationship between the rational part of the brain and the 'non-rational', emotions, faiths, and beliefs swirling in the mind that guide human behaviour. The elephant is a huge beast. The rider would like it to obey his orders. It is not easy, though. The rider must accept going with the elephant too, or else he will be thrown off entirely.

Economists are expanding their notions of how human beings make economic decisions. To rational intelligence, economists have now added emotional intelligence, as well as social intelligence, as intelligences that human beings use to determine what is the right thing to do. George

Akerlof, an economics' Noble Laureate, says that people's identities also shape the economic decisions they make (*Identity Economics: How our Identities Shape our Work, Wages, and Well-Being*, George Akerlof and Rachel Kranton). It seems that economists are realising that human beings are not merely 'rational, self-interested' beings. Perhaps it is time for economists to humbly admit that the foundations of many of the economic models they have been propounding are unsound and policy-makers should not follow them!

Haidt expands the foundations of moral codes. "Doing unto others as you would have done unto yourself" is a golden rule of morality, founded on the principles of 'causing no harm' and 'fairness'. However, many moral codes of societies relate to actions which an individual may want to do because he or she wants to, and which may not cause harm to anyone else. Nevertheless, such actions may be sanctioned in society. For example, personal dietary preferences, such as eating non-kosher food, or pork, or beef, are taboos in many societies. And disrespect of religious symbols or the desecration of national emblems can provoke moral outrage in strongly nationalist or religious societies—even if these acts are done in private.

Morality has five foundations, Haidt says. In addition to 'harm' and 'fairness', morality is also founded on the basic principles of 'loyalty', 'respect for authority', and 'sanctity'. He distinguishes between 'socio-centric' and 'individualistic' moral codes. Individualistic (or ego-centric) moral codes emphasise the rights of individuals—to 'be themselves', and 'to do their own thing'. Whereas socio-centric moral codes are founded on other principles too.

An individualist moral code is the basis for liberal economic as well as liberal social ideologies. 'Me' values came into prominence in the 1970s, with the hippy movements in the US and Europe. 'Me' values were also endorsed by economic theories founded on notions of purely rational and self-interested human beings that came to the fore in economics around the same time. The rise of excessively liberal ideas pushed aside deep-seated 'old fashioned' yearnings for values of loyalty, authority, and sanctity that people also have.

Loyalty, authority, and sanctity are socio-centric values. They honour the collective values of a group of people—a tribe, a religious community, and a nation. Individuals help a group to maintain its cohesion and its strength by honouring the values others in the group have. Individuals must realise that their own health depends on the health and sustainability of the society in which they live. An excessively individualist moral code can be destructive of society.

This explains the visceral reaction, even hatred, that religious people, and 'nationalists' too, have towards 'liberal' thinkers and anti-religious 'secularists' as well as anti-religious 'communists'. They see liberals, secularists, and communists as 'amoral' people.

Conservatives and liberals may use the same words to say what they value. However, the concepts and meanings behind the words they use can be very different. For example, both Republicans and Democrats in the US say they respect 'family values'. However, they see family values very differently, as George Lakoff, the American cognitive linguistic and philosopher, had eloquently explained in 1995, in his book, *Moral Politics: How Liberals and Conservatives Think*.

In the conservative model of a good family, fathers and mothers have distinct roles. Fathers must provide for the family and protect it. Mothers must care for the well-being of all the family's members. Children must respect their parents. Conservative families are caring and disciplined families. In the liberal model of a family also, parents care for their children. But parents' roles are more fluid in the liberal model, and children are given more space to express themselves and to develop in their own ways. Fairness, as well as doing no harm to others, are moral foundations for both types of families. Whereas, respect for authority, loyalty to one's family and nation, and the principle of sanctity (respecting religious and national symbols, for example), are stronger moral foundations for conservative families than for liberals.

Within every person is an elephant, and also a rider who tries to tame the elephant. The rider tries to be cool and calculating and to reason. But the elephant has a mind of its own, and feelings and moods, which often the rider cannot understand. It is not easy to have 'reasonable' conversations between people whose elephants cannot get on with each other.

Haidt provides another insight: the rider very often operates like the elephant's 'in house press secretary'. He (or she) is trying to find rational justifications for what the elephant instinctively believes in and does. Both, to justify the elephant's instinctive actions to others, and also to justify the actions in his (or her) own mind.

Peter Drucker, the great management philosopher of the 20th century, had consulted with CEOs of the largest companies in the world, and with Presidents of countries too. He said that whenever he met an important person, he would always ask for the person's opinions first, and not facts. Because any smart person, he said, knows how to find facts that will support his or her opinions. Our beliefs determine what facts we will accept, because within the human mind the elephant is more powerful than the rider. The 'Google world' of the 21st century, Haidt points out, makes it much easier for the 'press secretary' to find the 'alternative facts' that will support the chief's opinions. Googling makes it easier for both, the internal press secretary within each of us, as well as the President's official press secretary!

A great expectation of the internet was that, by enabling people everywhere to connect with people anywhere, it would bring people closer together. Whereas, the world is becoming more divided by the technologies applied by social media platforms which give people the facts they prefer and make connections for them with people they 'like'. The Big Data analysis that empowers Google and social media platforms such as Facebook and Twitter is the knowledge of people's preferences these platforms sell to advertisers (and even to political parties as the Cambridge Analytica scandal revealed). Thus, the elephants within us are being herded into virtual corrals, of 'people like us' separated from 'people not like us'. People within these corrals listen only to others in the same ideological corrals. They shut out the views of people in other moral and ideological corrals, even when they live together in the same countries, the same towns, and sometimes even in the same houses.

The big shock for many Americans with the election of Donald Trump was how viscerally divided Americans had become. They live in the same country and are governed by the same Constitution. Yet they have very different visions of what makes their country great. In India too, divisions are sharpening amongst people, about their visions of what will make India great. Will India, a richly diverse country, with many 'different elephants in the room'—people with many traditions and many religions—be a country in which people will relish its diversity? Or, will one tradition and one religion shut out others?

PART 3: A DIALOGUE AMONGST ELEPHANTS

Conversations amongst the rational riders of elephants could be conducted in facts-based, data-rich, quantitative language. Technology can make such conversations more efficient. However, there is a real danger, as Ellenberg pointed out in his book, *How Not to be Wrong*, that, by strengthening our abilities to analyse some questions mathematically, we acquire a general confidence in our beliefs, which extends unjustifiably to those things we're still wrong about.

Unlike debates amongst riders, dialogues amongst elephants must delve into worlds of emotions and beliefs that lie deep beneath the world of mathematical rationality. The mental processes of elephants are influenced by moral matrices, which combine several moral principles in varied combinations. The matrices are formed by processes of social evolution deep within the human psyche. They are shaped by the cultures of the families and societies in which human beings grow.

The title of my essay was a question: Who will robots and elephants vote for: Donald Trump or Xi Jinping? To answer this, one must know what sort of world robots and elephants want to live in. Robots powered with AI may prefer a more mechanically efficient and predictable world, because that is what they are most comfortable in, according to the authors of *Prediction Machines: The Simple Economics of Artificial Intelligence*. However, human beings, who have more of the wisdom of elephants in them than the rationality of robots, may prefer a different world, rich in emotional interactions amongst diverse people, all of whom have freedom to evolve and grow in their own ways.

I included Donald Trump and Xi Jinping in the title of my essay as strawmen for different political systems. The US system is a noisy democracy, in which people have the rights to be themselves and to speak up against their leaders. The Chinese system values order: in it, authority must be respected. A moot question is: which is the better society? Both societies need citizens to follow the 'rules of the game' so that their societies can provide them with 'what their country should do for them' (twisting John F. Kennedy's memorable appeal a little bit).

In a democratic society in which citizens want individual freedom and resent any dictatorial power over themselves, but want social order too, the citizens must be able to reconcile their diverse preferences amongst themselves. Therefore, a good democracy cannot rely only on *vertical processes* of democracy, of voting upwards to choose the leader citizens want.

Because then the elections will divide them along the lines of the type of society, and the values of the leader they choose, as has happened in the US, and is happening in many democratic countries in Europe too. Good democracies need sound *lateral* processes for deliberations amongst citizens, for people to listen to each other, and come to agreements about the fundamental rules of the game they will accept.

A dialogue amongst people must be a dialogue amongst the elephants within us. It cannot be limited to debates about facts. Elephants must also understand each other's beliefs. Haidt suggests an anti-dote to the self-righteous indignation, aggravated by social media technologies, that is messing up discourse amongst people. He says, "If you want to open your mind, open your heart first. If you have at least one friendly interaction with a member of the 'other' group, you'll find it far easier to listen what they are saying, and maybe even see a controversial issue in a new light."

Listening seems such a simple solution, too simple perhaps to solve the complex problems humanity must solve: rapid environmental degradation, persistent inequities, social divisiveness, and challenges in regulating technologies that are getting ahead of human capacities to manage them. These problems have many contributory causes, and they require cooperative action amongst diverse people with expertise in different areas, and amongst people with different ideologies too. People must be willing and able to listen to each other so that, by combining their knowledge, they can, like the blind men around the proverbial elephant see the whole elephant.

We must learn to listen to people who are not like us, and whom we may not even like. Sadly, with the barrage of bits of information from our always on smartphones, we are losing the art of listening when we must learn to listen to each other more deeply.

The first level of listening is to pay attention to 'what' the other person is saying, even if one does not agree. The instinct of a debater is to get ready with a riposte to prove the other wrong. Therefore, a debater stops listening even while the other is speaking.

Unlike a good debater, a good listener listens well to what the other is saying and also 'listens' to her own mind's reactions to it. She notices her disagreement, and her desire to counter the other. But she stops herself and goes into a second and deeper level of listening. At this level, she wonders 'why' the other thinks the way he does. And, rather than debate the other, she asks the other, with genuine interest, 'why do you believe what you do?' Thus, she begins to inquire into another's way of thinking. And begins to see the 'lens' through which the other sees the world.

From this second level, deep listeners come to a third, even deeper level of listening. At this level, the listener begins to notice the difference between her own way of seeing the world and the other's. Thus, she may begin to see her own lens. Our lenses are our ways of seeing and thinking. They are buried within the backs of our heads. We cannot see them with our own eyes. However, we may see them reflected in the eyes of another. Deep listening makes one aware of 'who' another is. Deep listening also brings self-awareness, of who I am.

The question, 'What sort of world are we leaving for our grandchildren?' has become a cliché. We cannot continue to live as we are and leave it to our children to produce a more inclusive, more just, more harmonious, and more sustainable world for our grandchildren.

We must change, and we must collaborate with others to shape our collective future. Let us listen to our own aspirations. We must listen also to the aspirations of people not like us for the better world they want to leave for their grandchildren.

(This essay was published by Founding Fuel in September 2018)

6

Who Do Economists Serve Really?

Mainstream economic theories do not fit reality. Two new books, 'Measuring What Counts' and 'Good Economics for Hard Times', provide a counterview: Instead of treating people as data, listen to them, and find answers to their real problems for inclusive, sustainable progress

A person walking at night sees a man searching for something under a lamppost, in an old Sufi story. The man says he is searching for his keys. The passer-by begins to search along with the man, then stops and asks if he is sure he lost them there. The man replies, no, he lost them in the park. The passer-by is incredulous. "Why then are you searching for them here?" he asks. "Because it is dark in the park and there is light here," the man replies.

A few Nobel laureates say that their fellow economists should step out of their discipline's limited circle of light if they want to find the keys to the complex issues that policymakers must grapple with. Joseph Stiglitz (who won the Nobel Prize in 2001), Jean-Paul Fitoussi and Martine Durand, provide a view from the policy-makers cockpit in *Measuring What Counts: The Global Movement for Well-Being*. It follows on from an earlier book, *Mismeasuring Our Lives—Why GDP Doesn't Add Up* published by Stiglitz and Fitoussi, along with Amartya Sen, another Nobel laureate, in 2010. Abhijit Banerjee and Esther Duflo, who won the Nobel Prize for economics in 2019 with Michael Kramer, provide a ground-up perspective in *Good Economics for Hard Times—Better Answers to Our Biggest Problems*.

These books combine top-down and bottom-up perspectives like Yin and Yang. Each includes the other perspective within it. Reading them together has provided an intellectual feast this holiday season. *Measuring What Counts* is focused on national score-cards— gauges for the pilots to steer the passengers aboard to where they want to go. Governments and economists must understand citizens' aspirations much better, it says. Because, "The objective of economics and social progress is to increase people's well-being. Who knows better than people themselves how well off they are and what most affects their lives? Money isn't everything in life…"

Banerjee and Duflo, who have been recognized for their work in the poorest communities of India and Africa, concur. Human dignity must be restored to its central place in economic policies, they say. Macro-economists treat people as data—as numbers in their equations—to answer the 'scientific' questions that economists have. Both books urge economists and policymakers to listen to the people whose welfare must be improved. Economists should understand the questions real people have and use their tools to help people find answers to their real problems.

Both books venture out of the lamplight of mainstream economics. They search for the keys to more inclusive and sustainable progress in a real world of real people. The first sentence in *Measuring What Counts* is, "The world is facing three existential crises: a climate crisis, and inequality crisis, and a crisis in democracy". "Economics is too important to be left to economists", is the very last sentence in *Good Economics for Hard Times— Better Answers to Our Biggest Problems.*

Economics' Holy Cows

Eighty-four individuals have been awarded the Nobel prize in economics. Only two are women. Duflo is the second. The first was Elinor Ostrom who won the prize in 2009 for her work on community governance of shared resources. Duflo's work—like Ostrom's—has been grounded in communities. Duflo, Banerjee, and Kramer won the Nobel Prize for using the tools of 'randomized control trials' to understand how socio-economic systems actually work on the ground to improve delivery of health and education services, for example.

"It seems a large part of the general public has entirely stopped listening to economists about economics," Duflo and Banerjee say. They add, "We, the economists...sometimes forget where science ends and ideology begins." Their book traces the evolution of mainstream economics' theories. And explains why they do not fit reality.

Free trade

One is the theory of free trade. That it will lift all boats. Which is founded on the logic of competitive advantage. It says if every nation produces what it can produce better than everyone else and bought from other nations what they can produce best, the whole world will be better off. Because global resources will be most optimally used. So, with the same resources, more will be produced overall. Therefore, free trade increases global efficiency.

This model ignores the complex process of transition—of going from a point where nations may already be producing some things that others can produce better than them to the point where they have given up production of these to produce more of what they theoretically can produce better than others' can. (And who must also give up production of what they produce and make something else.) During the transition, there will have to be a large shuffling around among countries, and within countries, of people giving up what they are doing to do something else.

Economists' theories of free trade are stripped of social realities, say Banerjee and Duflo. Who explain the 'stickiness' of socio-economic systems. Jobs are only one part of a human being's life, albeit an important one. Jobs are embedded within complex social realities—of community life and family responsibilities. Therefore, people cannot just 'up and go' somewhere else when the process of 'creative destruction' demands they give up their jobs for something else. Even a change to another profession within the same community—if the new jobs are within the same locality—takes time. New skills must be learned. During that process too, family obligations have to be fulfilled. The process of shuffling around is messy and takes a long time. So, while free trade may increase GDP in the long run, it will produce many winners and losers during the transition. And transitions could take a generation or two or even more.

When trade opens across borders, some sections of society benefit before others can. With volumes of trade increasing, traders will benefit first. Whereas, makers of products which were produced domestically but are now imported will take a long time to recover their levels of incomes—if they can. When they express their pain, they are labelled as anti-trade retrogrades who don't want progress. Trade economists have focused on the size of the pie. They have tended to stay away from thinking about how the pie is shared. Dani Rodrik, another economist who has also challenged some holy cows of economics, has estimated that for every dollar increase in the size of the global pie with free trade, six or seven dollars' worth of production and incomes will have to be shuffled around within countries.

When advocates of free trade also propound that governments should get out of the way and leave it to the market to facilitate the necessary adjustments in people's lives, citizens become convinced that neither economists nor their governments understand or care about them. "The gap between the 'experts' and the citizen they are supposed to be serving has played an important role in the bitter divisions within society that have been so visibly demonstrated in a number of recent elections," Stiglitz and his co-authors say.

Markets

The second holy cow is worship of markets. Unrestrained markets are the solution to everything for many economists, including the provision of public services. 'Get government out of the way: leave it to the market', they urge. Their diagnosis of the slow growth of jobs and incomes and slow-down in India's GDP growth is: India has not opened to international trade enough, and has not reformed its land and labour markets sufficiently.

Free trade and markets are not a panacea, Duflo and Banerjee explain. They refer to a study by Petia Topalova, a Ph.D. student at MIT, who studied the impact of India's massive trade liberalization of 1991 on various parts of the country over the next 20 years. The national average poverty rate declined from 35% to 15% which is impressive (though it cannot be attributed only to trade liberalization). What Topalova found was that the *more* exposed a particular district was to international trade, the *slower* poverty reduction was in that district. Moreover, the incidence of child labour dropped *less* in districts more exposed to trade than in the rest of the country. Whereas districts *less* exposed to international trade had prospered faster.

The reaction in the economics profession to her findings was surprisingly brutal, Banerjee and Duflo note. How could trade actually increase poverty? The theory tells us trade is universally good for the poor in poor countries so her data must be wrong. She was blackballed by the academic elite.

Banerjee and Duflo explain that the slow improvement of welfare with free trade was due to the complex compositions of socio-economic clusters and their 'stickiness'. Tight clusters are fertile grounds for innovation, entrepreneurship, and growth. They are fertile because they combine diverse resources through many economic as well as social interactions within the cluster. The stickiness which makes them fertile makes them resistant to being shaken up too.

The concept of a market for labour is controversial. 'Labour' is provided by human beings. Commodities can be bought and sold in markets. Humans are not commodities to be traded for prices determined by supply and demand, which they were in the slave trade. But that era should have passed entirely. Humans are not fodder for an economic machine to increase its GDP. They must be the principal beneficiaries of the growth of GDP. Economists must be reminded, says Stiglitz, that the purpose of economic growth is to improve the well-being of humans.

Human beings have the ability to learn and improve their own capabilities. Which, commodities do not have. Nor have machines so far. Machines will in the future with advances in artificial intelligence and robotics. Until then, humans are the only component of the production system that can improve its own productivity. It can improve the 'total factor productivity' of the whole system also with innovations in the utilization of machines and reductions in use of materials and energy.

Humans are stripped of their humanity when, in economists' mathematical equations of resources and outputs, 'labour' appears as an input like any other. They become 'objects' to be counted and measured; and to be discarded if they have no apparent value for the economic process. Henry

Ford I, a pioneer in the application of ideas of efficiency and scale in mass production systems, complained that when he wanted only a pair of hands, he had to suffer a whole human being with emotions and demands for justice.

Humans are not commodities; nor are they just labour; or disembodied technology. They are creatures with memories of their histories, an awareness of their identities, and emotions, fears, and aspirations. These powerful, non-*homo economicus,* forces have been known for millennia to philosophers and poets who have researched them and written about them. Only recently have mainstream economists begun to include emotions and identity into their calculus.

A labour 'market' is not an economic construct only. It has social and power dimensions too. The aim of labour market reforms must be to improve the well-being of human beings who provide their labour, not just make it easy for employers to buy and sell—'hire and fire'—workers, like they can buy and sell other inputs in their enterprises.

Economics' ideology changed after the Great Depression in the last century. Keynes advocated a larger role for governments in stimulating economic growth with public investments that create employment. Governments built large social security nets for citizens. The shift of economic policies towards citizens' welfare with larger government was supported by more taxation of those who could pay, i.e. wealthier citizens and corporations.

Ideology changed again in the 1970s. The ideology of free markets spread from the Chicago School into economics and into politics. Margaret Thatcher was its first powerful proponent. Then Ronald Regan declared, 'Government is not the solution; it is the problem.' In this ideology, taxation of the rich was a drag on economic growth. Their 'animal spirits'—their greed to make more money—must be released, urged the economists. When the rich make more money, the benefits will trickle down to the people below.

Economic inequalities within societies have increased since then, Thomas Piketty, Oxfam, and many others point out. All boats seem to have been lifted with the rising tide. But, with the financialization of economies and reduction of taxes on wealth, some boats have become airplanes taking the wealth of the top 0.1% in them into the stratosphere. And some boats, in poorer countries, did not lift at all. The desperation of these people to escape from hopelessness made them risk their lives on boats to richer countries. They were turned away because many citizens in those countries felt they were not well off. They were losing their jobs with the 'creative destruction' of free markets. Their governments could not step in to help them. Their governments' policies seemed to be dictated by financial institutions, supported by the economics' ideology that less government and more privatization of assets was the best solution.

When the global financial crisis spread around the world destroying many livelihoods citizens rose up in many countries. They were angry that governments were protecting financial institutions, and not them. President Nicolas Sarkozy of France set up a commission, chaired by Stiglitz, Sen, and Fitoussi, to recommend what must be changed in government policies to improve the welfare of citizens. To whom heads of governments, especially elected ones, must be principally accountable, rather than to financial investors. The commission published its report, *Mismeasuring Our Lives*, in 2010.

Measuring What Counts is written nine years later. Stiglitz and his co-authors provide evidence that tax reductions for the wealthy did not contribute much, if anything, to overall economic growth since the financial crisis—or even previously in economic history. On the other hand, tax reductions have been a principal cause of rising inequalities, and also the declining trust of citizens in their governments and in the motives of capitalists. Banerjee and Duflo say, "Bad economics underpinned the grand give-aways to the rich and the squeezing of welfare programmes, and sold the idea that the state is impotent and corrupt...and paved the way to the current stalemate of exploding inequality."

Stiglitz begins *Measuring What Counts* with the observation that, in spite of so much evidence to the contrary, not much seems to have changed in the paradigm of government policies, and the ideologies of economists around them, for taxation of the rich and welfare of those not well off. Scientific paradigms can be sticky, Thomas Kuhn explained in his seminal book, *The*

Structures of Scientific Revolutions. New ideologies threaten those who rose to social acclaim and to political power on the backs of ruling ideologies.

What to Measure and How to Measure

"[Our] central message is that what we measure affects what we do. If we measure the wrong thing, we will do the wrong thing. If we don't measure something, it becomes neglected, as if the problem didn't exist," say the authors of *Measuring What Counts*.

Stiglitz and his co-authors recommend improvements of the gauges used by the pilots and the navigators in the cockpit of economic policymaking—government leaders and the experts who guide them.

1. Measure the shape of the system, not the size of the economy

"There is no simple way of representing every aspect of well-being in a single number in the way GDP describes market economic output. We need to move 'beyond GDP' when assessing a country's health," say the authors of *Measuring What Counts*.

No good physician would gauge the health of a human body by its size. The physician wants to know what is going on inside. She will use many diagnostic instruments to look inside, and require many pathological tests to assess how well the internal processes are functioning. She will want to see all reports, not their mathematical conversion into a single number. Then only can she gauge which organ in the body has become unhealthy. With their preference for a single number—GDP, and that too a measure of the size of the economy—economists disable themselves from prescribing good policies to improve an economy's health.

The Indian economy is going through a 'measurement crisis'. Employment and incomes' trends reported by Indian statistical agencies, which do not show a healthy economy, are denied by the government. And the size of the GDP reported by the government is doubted by economists!

The Indian government and its spokespersons in the media and in business harp only on the goal of a $5 trillion economy—as if it will be the panacea for all the environmental, social, and economic problems ailing the country. How then can the citizens trust the government to find the right solutions?

2. Why the obsession with only one number?

Stiglitz and his co-authors laud the evolution of the 17 Sustainable Development Goals because they broaden the measurement framework and add more gauges. At the same time they worry that there may be too many numbers to enable comparisons across countries.

Single numbers make it easier to rank countries. Rankings attract attention. They spur losers to overtake the winners. Therefore rankings spur progress. The derivation of a single number from many measures of disparate conditions requires weights to be assigned to them. Which is not easy. How much weightage should a physician give to the heart, the brain, the liver, the kidneys, etc. in an assessment of human health? Is it necessary at all for determining which needs attention most? Surely, what needs attention would depend on the condition of that specific patient at that specific time.

It is more useful to display all the gauges side-by-side to make an all-round assessment. The OECD's *"How's Life?—Assessment of the Comparative Strengths and Weaknesses in Current Levels of Well Being"* framework presents data about 11 indicators for each country, which include 'Income and Wealth', 'Subject Well-Being', 'Environmental Quality', 'Civic Engagement and Governance', and seven others. They are presented in a 'spider diagram' form within a circle. Thus one may, at one glance, see the *shape* of the system. Which is the weakest organ in the country? Civic Engagement and Governance? Or, Income and Wealth?

Economists must develop frameworks for measurement and presentation of information that don't squish complex shapes into a single number. The shapes of complex systems are better determinants of their health than are their sizes.

3. Missing capital

Stiglitz points to a deficiency in national accounts. They include only financial capital and natural resources as assets of the economy. They should include human capital and social capital as assets too. Because these are the founts of innovation and productivity.

Productivity of countries when measured in the conventional way—which is output per person in the country—can be improved by reducing the denominator in the equation, i.e. the numbers of persons in the country. Restrict immigrants; reduce birth rates. However, immigrants add numbers and variety to human resources. More young people bring more new energy to human capital. Declining human resources, with reductions in birth rates and restrictions on immigration, in Japan and other economically rich countries is dampening their economic growth.

More people can add to human capital. However, the number of people is not a sufficient measure of human capital. The quality of their health and education matters too. Indian economists, who projected that India would obtain a 'demographic dividend' because it has a large population of young people—as China had when its economy took off—have realized that the neglect of public health and school education (while they pressed the government to focus on GDP growth) has weakened India's growth story.

A common saying, "First increase the size of the pie before it is shared with the people", misses an essential requirement for economic growth. People are the *means* for increasing the size of the pie, and not merely *beneficiaries* of a large pie made for them.

4. Trust

Measuring What Counts emphasises the importance of social capital. It is 'the glue that holds society together', the authors say.

Social capital is a fuzzy, and essential, ingredient for growth and well-being. The report focuses its attention on one aspect of social capital, albeit a very important one—*trust*. "We should think of trust as an asset, as a key part of social capital," it says. It defines trust as "a person's belief that another person or institution will act consistently with their expectations of positive behaviour." Not surprisingly, trust is related to subjective well-being. For instance, cooperative social relationships with others, which are facilitated by trust and give rise to trust, affect people's health and happiness above and beyond the monetary gains derived from cooperation.

Lack of trust has grave political consequences, the authors point out. Growing economic insecurity and higher unemployment lower trust in political institutions. This in turn leads to higher voting for populist parties, a noticeable trend in many countries.

The authors explain that actions and processes that are *perceived* to be "unfair" (for instance, in how people are treated in the processes by which decisions get made) undermine trust. In the United States the seemingly favourable treatment given to bankers, relative to that given to homeowners, undermined trust in government. So too in Europe, where the austerity measures imposed on crisis countries—with particularly adverse effects on the poor—were widely perceived as unfair, undermining trust in the key European institutions.

While research on the causes and consequences of trust is still in its infancy, it is proving to be a rich field of endeavour, the authors say, with promising insights into understandings of economic performance and social progress. From studies so far it can be concluded that countries with higher levels of trust tend to have higher per capita income. Another finding is that trust is negatively correlated with income inequality. And rising income inequality has also been related to lower trust in institutions.

"To date, we still have an imperfect understanding of causality, and indeed, causality may often run in both directions," the authors observe. A lack of trust in public institutions may hamper their ability to engage in redistribution because there may be a fear that redistribution will go the wrong way, i.e., from the poor to the rich. But high levels of inequality, especially when they cannot be justified, also undermine trust in institutions. Similarly, a well-functioning legal system may enhance trust, while a lack of trust may lead to an overly rule-bounded legal system in which, in the process of following detailed rules, miscarriages of justice may end up undermining trust.

Trust takes time to build but can dissipate quickly when people perceive that others did not behave in a trustworthy way. When institutions are dysfunctional and the rules of the game are perceived as unfair, they lower people's willingness to cooperate with each other, creating a "society of mistrust". Good measures of trust have been lacking, and this has contributed to policymakers' failure to focus adequately on trust. Given the importance of trust, policymakers should pay more attention to it, and to how their policies affect it.

Science advances when scientists sense that something is missing in their understanding of how the system works. Then they focus on it, understand what it is, and develop ways to measure it. Newton sensed there was a universal force that brought down everything that went up. Then he hypothesised what this force could be. And he experimented and measured it.

The pursuit of numbers, in the belief that numbers alone indicate accuracy, has become the bane of economics. Many forces that shape societies and economies cannot be easily measured such as the trust of citizens in institutions. Such substantial forces must not be excluded from a model which seeks to explain the behaviour of the economy. Robert Lucas, who received the Nobel Prize in economics for expounding the 'rational-expectations' view of human behaviour, referred to a theory as something that can be put on a computer and run. Many economists insist on equations and numbers because that is all that computers can compute, whereas economists should study human behaviour as it is, not as they find easy to model.

Learning and Listening

How do economists learn about how societies function? And, how do societies learn to improve themselves? These are fundamental questions running through both books.

Stiglitz and Bruce Greenwald examined how societies learn in *Creating a Learning Society: A New Approach to Growth, Development, and Social* (published in 2014). They looked at the process of industrialisation, which has been the principal driver of economic growth for countries.

Economies grow and living standards improve when countries move from agriculture and resource extraction to use machines to produce things they were producing with only labour—such as textiles, and move on to producing more complex things they could not produce before—such as automobiles.

An invention of a new product in a laboratory is not sufficient. The conversion of the idea into products that are sold and serviced, and bought and used creates new jobs and growth. Many people and many institutions must learn to do what they could not do before, and learn together. Some people must learn to operate machines they had never seen before. And others must learn how to make those machines! Managers must learn to manage more complex production systems. And governments must evolve their abilities to support and regulate activities they had not done before. All must learn, and learn to work together too, for the country to develop a competitive industrial capability.

All countries that have industrialised have taken this path of learning. Those that learned faster overtook those that had industrialised before them. They became more competitive. Thus, by focusing on learning and systems improvements on the shop-floor, and by learning how to coordinate actions across government ministries, in cooperation with industries—the vaunted MITI (Japan's Ministry of International Trade and Industry) and 'Japan Inc'—overtook the West in many industries.

Many factors, and many actors, combine to create the complex capabilities required for industrial development and for the development of good educational and health systems too. Many must learn, and they must learn together, to understand the system of which they are a part. They must also learn to self-govern as a system. Elinor Ostrom, the first woman to get the Nobel Prize in economics was awarded for her work in community self-governance. Esther Duflo, the second, has also been awarded for the study of local systems (along with Banerjee and Kramer). 'Sticky clusters' are institutions essential for improvement and growth.

The first 16 of the 17 Sustainable Development Goals name the challenges humanity must find solutions to, faster. They range across a spectrum of environmental and social issues—from climate change, economic growth, to inequity. These challenges are manifested in different combinations in different countries. And, indeed, they appear differently in different parts of countries. Therefore, the solutions to them must fit local realities. 'One-size fits all' solutions will not achieve the SDGs. *Local systems solutions are the way to solve global systemic problems.*

The 17th goal is 'partnerships'. Here is the solution to the dilemma Stiglitz alludes to—about too many measurements in the SDGs. Every community—a country, or a state, a city, or a village—is a system. The stakeholders within each system must map the relevant conditions in the system of which they are a part. They must understand the interactions among these forces, and see what actions they could take to improve their condition. Communities themselves can be the greatest beneficiaries of Randomised Control Trials conducted at community levels for which Banerjee, Duflo, and Kramer have been recognized. The trials provide insights that can empower communities. With a better understanding of what matters, they can negotiate with the larger system around them, and with the governance system above them, for what they really need.

A moral question for economists is, who do they serve? Stiglitz says that 'well-being' is subjective. It is difficult to understand objectively and to quantify. Are people objects, and merely data for scientists' equations? Or, should economists, and the policy-makers they guide with their science, listen more deeply to people to understand what really matters to them?

A Final Philosophical Question

Economists are envious of the precision with which physicists can predict the phenomena they study. Physicists are realising there may be limits to what they can know. Heisenberg's Principle of Uncertainty, a seminal proposition in physics, states that observations will change what is observed. Moreover, in quantum physics, it is not possible to know everything about a particle exactly. The observer can either know its position or the speed of its motion.

Policymakers design measurement systems to manage the economy. They impose a 'form' on the system to make it easier for them to read it. People react to the ways in which they are measured, and the system changes its form. James C. Scott gives many examples in *Seeing Like a State: How Certain Schemes to Improve the Human Condition Have Falied*

France introduced the 'window tax' to make it easier for assessors to calculate property values. They had observed that the numbers of windows in a house correlated well with the size of the house. So, by walking around the house and counting the windows, an assessor could gauge the size of the house fairly well. He did not have to go in to measure the space.

Citizens reduced the number of windows on the houses they built to reduce their tax assessments. (Hence old French houses have fewer windows). Fewer windows resulted in poorly ventilated homes, which caused public health problems. The unintended consequence of an efficient measurement system was another problem for the state!

Physicists study inanimate matter and energy. The mind of the electron the physicist observes is different, and perhaps less complex than the mind of the physicist. To understand the behaviour of economies, which are social systems, not merely material systems, economists must understand human behaviour. The minds whose reasoning they must understand are as complex as their own.

Physician, first heal thyself, is wise counsel. The core message of both books is: economists must step out of the circle of lamplight of their own rationales and mathematical calculations. They should step out into the real world to listen to real people for whose well-being they must find better solutions.

(This essay was published by Founding Fuel in January 2020)

7

Why Is Economic Theory behind the Curve?

Nate Silver, the American statistician and writer, points out in *The Signal and the Noise* (2012), that forecasts of GDP growth since 1968 by the Survey of Professional Forecasters have been right only 50 per cent of the time—no better than tossing a coin. After the global financial crisis, Queen Elizabeth asked, at the London School of Economics, why hardly any economist had predicted the crash. British economist Adair Turner, delivering the 2010 Lionel Robbins Memorial Lectures, said the time has come to reconstruct economics. The question is, why is economics theory behind the curve, when many, including some economists, know that economics must change?

Economics is experiencing the pains of a paradigm shift. In his classic treatise, *The Structure of Scientific Revolutions*, Thomas Kuhn explains why paradigms are hard to change. In each science, whether physics, chemistry, biology, or astronomy, a core idea is adopted by its community, and all its experiments and theories are built around this idea. There are long periods of what Kuhn calls 'normal' science during which it is heresy to challenge this core idea. Anyone who does is ostracized by the scientific community.

Revolutions occur, he explains, when after many decades of accumulation of contrarian evidence, this idea is let go off and a new one replaces it. The process of learning of new paradigms must go along with the unlearning of old ones. For example, acceptance that the earth is not at the center of the universe, that matter has wave-like properties, and that species evolve, required the letting go of core beliefs to the contrary. Unlearning is not easy because vested interests in the established order will resist changes that diminish their importance.

Turner says, with a twist of Keynes' famous statement, that 'practical men, who believe themselves to be quite exempt from any intellectual influences, are usually the slave of some defunct economist'. Turner warns that 'the great danger lies with the reasonably intellectual men and women who are employed in the policy-making departments—who tend to gravitate to the dominant beliefs of economists who are still very much alive.' Economists have acquired greater power than any other academic discipline to shape national and international policies. They are sitting on a pedestal they do not want to get off.

James Galbraith says, in *The End of Normal: The Great Crisis and the Future of Growth,* that economists have redefined human experience into a special language limited to concepts that could be dealt with inside their established model. A core idea of the prevalent paradigm of economics is: humans are rational, self interested beings. Another core idea driving economic policies is: markets must be made free to enable self-interested individuals and corporations to fulfill their material aspirations and produce more economic growth. Galbraith says, 'Any refusal to shed the larger perspective—a stubborn insistence on bringing a broader set of facts or a different range of theory to bear—identifies one as "not an economist". In this way, economists need only talk to one another. Enclosed carefully in their monastery, they can speak their code, establish their status rankings and hierarchies, and persuade themselves and one another of their intellectual and professional merit.' Thus, echoing Kuhn, Galbraith describes symptoms of a science stuck in an old normal.

Economists, envying the power of physicists, who develop theories with which they can make very accurate predictions, have become too much enamored of numbers. Robert Lucas, who received the Nobel Prize in economics for expounding the 'rational expectations' view of human behavior, referred to a theory as something that can be put on a computer and run. Many economists insist on equations and numbers because that is all that computers can compute, whereas economists should study human behavior as it is, not as as they find easy to model.

Isaiah Berlin says in his treatise, *'On Political Judgement':*

"All socially engineered systems of formal order are in fact subsystems of a larger system on which they are ultimately dependent, not to say parasitic. The subsystem relies on a variety of processes—frequently informal and antecedent—which alone it cannot create or maintain. The more schematic, thin, and simplified the formal order, the less resilient and more vulnerable it is to distortions outside its narrow parameters."

Human beings and social systems are driven by emotions, egos, and desires for dignity and power—drivers that are not easy to quantify, but must figure in any accurate model of reality. Historians and other social scientists have been studying these forces for a hundred years and more. Economists had stripped them out of their computable models, and were slipping behind other social disciplines in their ability to explain reality. Now some economists, with their recent treatises on the roles of identity and emotions in the decisions that people make (e.g. George Akerlof's *Identity Economics* and Richard Thaler's *Misbehaving: The Making of Behavioral Economics*), are stirring up uncomfortable debates amongst economists.

Economists are behind the curve because, as Kuhn explained, the letting go of an established paradigm in any science in the face of new evidence is not easy. Shifts in power, and egos and emotions, make it hard for rational people to endorse new ideas even when there is enough evidence. Perhaps some economist should try to model all the forces at play amongst economists, as economics lets go of its old 'normal' and struggles to acquire a new paradigm that can describe a world of normal humans.

(Blogpost August 2018)

8

The Gap between GDP and the SDGs

Two meetings on 7th May this year, only a few kilometres apart within Delhi, were conceptually in two different worlds. One was a meeting at the India International Centre (IIC) to commemorate the fiftieth anniversary of a seminal meeting held at the IIC in May 1966 on the social responsibilities of business. The meeting in 1966 was inaugurated by the Prime Minister of India, Lal Bahadur Shastri; the opening speech was delivered by the pre-eminent civil society leader Jaiprakash Narain; and the meeting ended with a Declaration of Business Responsibilities.

The other meeting on 7th May this year was at the Nehru Memorial Library, where Dr. Raghuram Rajan, governor of the Reserve Bank of India (RBI), delivered the 6th K.B. Lall Memorial Lecture. Dr. Rajan pointed out that the global economy is in the doldrums, and in a situation that it never has been in before. Economists have no prior experience of such a situation, he said, and they will have to invent solutions. He spoke at some length of the inaccuracies in conventional measurements of GDP, and their inappropriateness as measures of well-being of societies. However, at the end, the audience seemed to be most interested in whether the RBI would permit the publication of the names of the 500 corporate defaulters of loans from Indian banks. His remarks about this made the headlines of the national papers the next morning.

In the IIC, leaders of many civil society organizations described the damage to communities and the environment by corporations' products and production processes. They lamented that there had been barely any change in the behavior of corporations since the lofty conference on the social responsibilities of business 50 years ago. They said the 2% CSR law introduced by the Indian government was taking business backwards to an old paradigm of corporate social responsibility, associated with charity, wherein giving alms at the temple at the end of the week is absolution for any sins committed during the week while making money. What is really required, they asserted, is to make businesses accountable for the impacts their products, processes, and business practices have on society and on the environment, which the declaration of business responsibilities had already stated 50 years ago.

India's GDP may be growing. Not only were participants at the recent meeting at IIC skeptical about the numbers. They said GDP is the wrong metric of human progress. They were very angry with 'crony capitalists', who were subverting good governance, while becoming very rich themselves. In these matters, they seemed to be on the same page as the RBI governor, though saying the same things differently.

Dr. Rajan suggested that leaders of all countries' governments as well as heads of their central banks, need to coordinate amongst each other more closely, because the issues affecting global growth cross national boundaries. He proposed another Bretton Woods type conference, to create new rules and institutions to manage global financial and economic affairs. Whereas, all the matters the civil society organizations are concerned with—social development, environmental sustainability, and inequality of opportunities--are covered in the UN's Sustainable Development Goals (SDGs) that all countries' governments have agreed to last year.

The world is moving on two tracks which are not converging. On one track are institutions concerned with a narrowly defined 'economy', and with GDP. On the other track are institutions concerned with what GDP does not measure—environmental sustainability, human dignity, livelihoods, and justice—the concerns of the SDGs The two worlds of GDP and SDGs must come together.

The Bertelsmann Foundation of Germany has made a study of 'Winning Strategies for a Sustainable Future'. Bertelsmann studied 35 countries around the world that appear to be leaders in developing strategies for sustainable growth. Bertelsmann examined the quality of their strategies, the frameworks for implementation, and results so far. Bertelsmann selected five key success factors. Two of these must be highlighted because they are the starting points of the process of faster improvement.

The first is that sustainability policy derives from an overriding concept and guiding principles that are made to permeate significant areas of politics and society. And 'best practice' to make this happen is to get specific in national debates on a new score-card of progress. Inclusion and sustainability must be achieved along with growth. Therefore, balanced score-cards are being developed and used by leading nations.

The second requirement for success, Bertelsmann's study found, is that sustainability policy must be developed and implemented in a participatory manner. Therefore, the task for countries is to develop new participatory formats. Not only must large numbers of people be engaged, but different constituents must listen to each other to develop an integrative vision of the future of the country.

The global discourse, like the two meetings in Delhi, seems divided into two worlds: the world of finance and growth, and the world of equity and sustainability. Inhabitants of one world eat cake. In their world, one dollar equals one vote: those who have more money have a greater say in fixing the rules of the game. Inhabitants of the other world demand bread for everyone. In their world, one living body is one vote, regardless of how little it owns.

Increasing inequalities and crony capitalism are becoming issues of great concern agitating people everywhere. Economists too are concerned with the effects these issues have on economic growth. The anger against the established order is mounting. Donald Trump and Bernie Sanders have tapped into it in the USA. In India, unsatisfied demands for equal opportunities and fairness are fuelling unrest—by tribal people, farmers, and young people—in many parts of the country.

The world cannot carry on the way it is. Those inside the walls must enter into a dialogue with those outside the walls. The structure of the discourse must change. The two parallel discourses, about concerns with GDP and SDGs, must converge. It is no longer sufficient for finance ministers, central bank governors, and economists to talk amongst themselves to figure out solutions for the global economy. Civil society voices must participate in the dialogue too. These dialogues will be difficult initially. Mistrust is high.

Perspectives are different. Nevertheless, perspectives must be combined and trust built to improve the world for everyone.

Finally, social media is an inadequate platform for the meeting of minds required. It increases volumes and decibels in debates, and sharpens divisions. Whereas, deep dialogue to bridge divides requires, what Germans call 'four eye' conversations, in which two sets of human eyes look deeply into each other.

(Blogpost May 2016)

9

Movements of Change

I returned to hazardous pollution levels in India's National Capital Region last night. Last week I was immersed in a learning journey in spotlessly clean Singapore. Singapore is a remarkable country. Very small: 5 million people on a tiny island. It moved up from 'third world' levels of development to become a developed country within a few decades. A country to which people from even the most advanced Western countries now come to see how it works. In fact, I was included in the learning journey to Singapore by a German think-tank.

My first visits to Singapore were in the 1960s shortly after Singapore became an independent country. Then, remarkably, I was with a team from the Tata group in India, invited by the Singapore government not to learn but to teach Singapore: to teach Singaporeans how to develop skilled workers for the many Western MNCs that the government was inviting to invest in Singapore. Singapore has come a very long way since then. Comparatively, India is still at the starting blocks with miles to go yet for improving its own education and skill development systems.

How has Singapore learned and improved so fast? This was the question we explored on the learning journey. We met leaders in many institutions: the Lee Kuan Yew School of Public Policy, the Centre for Liveable Cities, the Lien Centre for Social Innovation, the School of Continuing Education and Lifelong Learning, the Centre for Artificial Intelligence, the Singapore Housing Board, and many others. On the side, with the help of a friend from India in Singapore, I met many students and faculty at the National University of Singapore (NUS) and the Singapore Management University, and at the 'consulting club' run by students, who were interested in ideas in my book, *Transforming Systems: Why the World Needs a New Ethical Toolkit*. Our learning journey concluded with a masterful wrap-up by Tharman Shanmugaratnam, Senior Minister and Coordinating Minister for Social Policies.

Local Solutions to Global Problems

Singapore is a small, land- and water-constrained country which is getting the most out of what it has by inducing all parts of the government and all stakeholders to work together. Singapore cannot have economies of scale comparable with other countries. Its remarkable progress is the result of an alternative approach—of harnessing 'economies of scope'. The dominant theory of management is to obtain economies through scale, by doing a few things on a large scale across a large geography. Which requires coordination at many levels—at the centre, in the middle and on the ground, of what these specialised organisations in business and in government do. The theory of 'economy of scope' says that complex systems produce better outcomes when coordination of their many different parts happens closer to the ground where outcomes are produced. Trade-offs between needs and resources are best adjusted on the ground closer to reality rather than in high-level meetings between many agencies.

Singapore officials say that, while they deploy digital technologies extensively and have adopted the globally fashionable term of 'smart cities', their thrust is to create 'liveable cities'. Therefore, coordination of service delivery is thrusted down to citizens, in community centres within the housing estates, where citizens are encouraged to participate in the governance of local schools, libraries and public health services, and are provided facilities to interact in sports and cultural activities and build a community spirit. Singapore illustrates very well the benefits of changing the dominant 'theory-in-use' in management and governance, from the prevalent one of 'global solutions to complex global problems' (in which complex problems are kicked upstairs to central governments and to the United Nations to solve), to an approach of 'local systems solutions to global systemic problems'.

Shanmugaratnam emphasised that more policy attention must be given to the needs of small enterprises, rather than large ones, to obtain inclusive growth. In *Transforming Systems*, I provide a systems' diagram of the 'circular economy' to explain the vital role that collective enterprises owned by small producers will play to reduce the increasing wealth inequalities in India and around the world.

Systems Thinking

Singapore is investing heavily in education all the way up from nursery schools to world class universities. What is noteworthy are the innovations in the education system to promote inter-disciplinary studies and develop the discipline of systems thinking. For example, undergraduates from various academic streams in NUS, ranging from science and economics to liberal arts, mingle in five colleges where they live, each with a cross-cutting theme of learning, such as systems thinking, community work, and social studies. They collaborate on college projects on these themes, in addition to their faculty's specialised curriculum.

My young guide was a fourth year student in economics, who belonged to the college that was focused on systems modelling. He was engaged with college mates from various disciplines to make a systems model of the causes and effects of population growth. He was delighted to see the diagram in my book, *Transforming Systems*, which combines cultural and economic determinants in population dynamics.

Eighty percent of Singapore's citizens live in homes leased to them by the government. However, the Singapore Housing Board sees its mission not merely as a providing of good housing, which it does very well. It describes its mission as building communities, to do which it must understand both sides of the housing system—its 'concrete' side, as well as its softer 'social' side too. It is continuously listening to the interplay between the two sides in its interactions with citizens. Thus, for example, it is continuously assessing whether the digital infrastructure it is building for communities provides the benefits the communities want.

Personally I was delighted, as Chairman of HelpAge International, to see how much attention is given to the needs and wants of the elderly in the design of digital facilities and services. The elderly are seen as a necessary part of a healthy, integrated inter-generational system, rather than as an economic burden to be taken care of in specialised facilities.

The Purpose of the Enterprise

Mark Zuckerberg's fall from grace is as remarkable as was his meteoric rise. From the young visionary in a college dorm, who invented a technological innovation with which billions of citizens all over the world could fulfil their social needs, he is being unmasked in the US Congress as a thick-skinned money-maker who is using citizens' personal data to make billions of dollars for himself and other financial investors in Facebook.

Singapore ranks very high on both, the ease of doing business by businesses, as well as the wellbeing and ease of living of its citizens. When Shanmugaratnam was asked how the Singapore government was balancing the needs of citizens with the demands of businesses, he said the government must be clear about its purpose, just as capitalist business enterprises are clear about theirs. All institutions are designed for a purpose.

The purpose of capitalist business enterprise is to make profits for investors and increase their wealth. A business corporation's governance is designed for this purpose, and its success is measured by how well it performs by its yardsticks. Whereas the purpose of governments, whatever their form—whether elected by universal franchise, or whether they are unelected, single party governments—is to fulfil the welfare and security needs of citizens. Business institutions are not designed to provide many social goods, nor should be expected to. Whereas governments must learn to provide these public goods if they cannot yet, and not pass on their responsibilities to the private sector, by privatising education and public health for example.

Business leaders are realising that they cannot stay stuck in the ideological rut that the business of business must be only business, which has driven the growth of economies around the world for the past forty years. When business leaders, such as the Business Roundtable in the US, try to break out of this paradigm, they are pushed back. *The Economist* has reminded them of their legally encased fiduciary responsibilities to their investors. These business leaders are good men and women trapped within institutional walls they cannot easily break out of.

Technologies are evolving rapidly, and institutions of government and business must evolve too. New concepts of 'social enterprises' and 'impact investing' are emerging. The ethics of a 'for profit' enterprise will be different to the ethics of an enterprise that is 'not-for-profit'. They respond to different societal needs. Is improvement of social wellbeing the core purpose of the enterprise? Or, is profit the underlying purpose of the enterprise masked beneath a veneer of social responsibility? If financial profit is only a means to the end, how should the fulfilment of the enterprise's core purpose be measured? Clearly, the success of the enterprise should not be measured by the financial size of a 'social enterprise' and its valuation when its investors exit it. Even though these are being adopted as surrogate measures of the success of social enterprises and impact investments.

'What we measure is what we get', is a fundamental principle of management. The consequences of measuring the performance of complex systems—corporations and even countries—with financial measures: profits and share values for corporations, and GDP for countries, is that non-monetisable (and non-quantifiable) qualities of systems, such as well-being of citizens, and fairness and justice, slip out of sight.

Platforms, Movements, and Networks

Platforms, movements, and networks fulfil different purposes. Technology has enabled the creation of platforms that provide enormous reach and that have reduced the costs of transactions. Amazon, Google, and Facebook are the most successful technology-enabled platforms. As for-profit enterprises, their success is evident in their huge valuations in the stock market and the wealth they have created for their promoters.

'Movements' are formations of large numbers of people who move together towards an objective. India's freedom movement, the civil rights movement in the US, and the Arab Spring were movements of people for a cause. They had a purpose to fulfil: to harness dispersed energies to topple an established order. No doubt, technology platforms have provided a very effective means for movements to organise themselves, as they did for the Arab Spring movements, for the citizens' protests in Hong Kong, and many other uprisings around the world. It is no surprise therefore that governments are very wary of the power provided by technology platforms to citizens' movements.

Platforms do not create movements: they only enable movements. A common purpose forms movements that may use platforms to amplify their power. A common purpose is central for the formation of movements and networks.

A distinction between movements and networks is worth noting. Movements are often *against something,* and they dissipate when the job is done—when the wall has been breached and the entrenched order has been toppled. However, the building of something new in place of what has been removed requires more sustained action and over longer periods of time. Movements arise to topple powerful organisations. Lacking any vision of an alternative form of organisation, they invariably replace one organisation with another similar one—one political party with another, one authoritarian government with yet another.

Whereas movements often require only the same capability from a large number of people—metaphorically all putting their shoulders to the wheel—all signing a petition, all squatting on the road, all donating a small sum of money, or all lighting a candle—networks require different forms of contributions and different capabilities to be combined to create something new in place of what has been removed.

Networks require sustained commitment from diverse participants to a common cause, the realisation of which cannot be marked by an event. Networks need more structures to coordinate an ongoing sharing of diverse resources, as well as more collaborative governance, than do movements.

A network is a different form of organisation—tighter than a movement, and looser than a hierarchical organisation. The architecture of strong networks follows the principles of 'complex self-adaptive systems' in nature. These are: permeable boundaries within and around them; minimal, critical rules for the management of their processes; diversity and flexibility in their resources; and aligned aspirations of their members. These rules are explained further in *Transforming Systems*.

The Purpose of our Lives

"Who am I? What is the purpose of my life? And, when will my life's work be done?" These are questions I have asked myself many times. I notice that many successful people, who have earned a lot of wealth through their innovations and investments, or earned well from success in professional careers in business and consulting, are asking themselves these questions. I am meeting many young people who are asking these questions much earlier in life before they have become rich and successful and have no wealth to 'give back'. They want to shape a better world for everyone.

The social and natural world of which we are all small parts, and the condition of which we are unhappy with, has been shaped by our ways of thinking and doing. As Albert Einstein is supposed to have said, to expect to solve the big problems we confront with the same thinking that created the problems is madness. These young people, as well as the older ones who want to make the world a better one for everyone, need a new toolkit. The new toolkit must be founded on new ways of thinking and being.

The new ethical toolkit I offer for their consideration, to young and old change-makers, in *Transforming Systems: Why the World Needs a New Ethical Toolkit*, is based on three new ways of thinking: ethical reasoning, systems thinking, and deep listening—especially to people not like us.

(Published by Founding Fuel in November 2019 with the title, Economies of scope: Singapore's alternative approach to progress)

10

Transforming Systems Is Key to Policy Gains

Two Indian initiatives have found places amongst the ten best global initiatives selected by the Rockefeller Foundation for its Food Systems Vision Prize 2050. One is the Nandi Foundation's work with tribal communities in Araku in South India. The other is 'Eat Right India', the countrywide movement for food systems change being shaped by the Food Safety and Standards Authority of India (FSSAI).

The capability to implement large scale change in complex systems is the key for India to realize the benefits of any well-thought policy or plan. The National Education Policy is the most recent example of a far-reaching policy wherein all commentators are concerned about how it will be implemented. Eat Right India, the only government-led initiative amongst the ten selected by the Rockefeller Foundation, has been examined by the World Bank to understand how a small government agency, with a limited budget, could induce systemic change in a complex subject like food availability and consumption. Eat Right India involves 1.3 billion consumers, and millions of tiny businesses—hawkers, food stall owners, farmers, and others, as well as multiple government stakeholders at the center and in the states.

Insights from the concept of Eat Right India and its implementation provide valuable insights into how large-scale change can be facilitated by a small government agency. Here are six key lessons.

1. A 'whole system' approach

Donella Meadows, who worked on the Club of Rome's report in the 1970s on 'the limits to growth', and who promoted systems thinking, pointed out that "every system is perfectly designed to produce the results *it is presently producing.*" Therefore, to understand what is required for India to Eat Right, one must begin by understanding why India is *not* eating right at present. In this way, the many causes, physical as well as behavioral, as well as the roles that many stakeholders are playing while satisfying their own interests, which together are producing undesirable outcomes for everyone, can be located.

2. Learn to listen well

The Harvard Kennedy School commends the power of listening for complex systems change. In its report, "Systems Leadership for Sustainable Development: Taking Action on Complex Challenges through the Power of Networks", it says:

"To change a complex system, stakeholders must first understand how the system works – the components, actors, dynamics, and influences that together create the system and its current outcomes. Most stakeholders have experienced and learned about the system from one point of view. Truly understanding its many dimensions requires absorbing new information and learning from other stakeholders' viewpoints and perspectives. This means constant dialogue, underpinned by radical and empathic listening, enabling each actor to have a deeper appreciation of the multiple perspectives on a particular system."

3. Catalysis, not control, for 'whole of government', multi-stakeholder collaboration

Broad systems change in any complex subject, such as food production and consumption, or education, or public health, requires many changes to be implemented at the same time. All cannot be the remit of one agency. Therefore, many agencies, and many stakeholders outside the government too, must cooperate. The nodal agency cannot be their controller: it must facilitate cooperation amongst them. Government officers (and even private sector managers) find this hard to do. 'Give me authority over the others, and the budget required, and I will get it done', they say. They do not know how to lead by influencing and enabling others.

4. The quality of a system cannot be changed by prescription and inspection

The conventional approach to regulation of a system is to lay down the rules that its participants must follow, and then inspect to ensure the rules are being followed. This approach can lead to too many rules and too many inspectors—the problem India is struggling to break out of to make it easier for businesses to do business. Industries often use this approach for their internal quality management too with engineers spelling out the processes and standards and inspectors checking to see if workers are following them.

Japanese industries adopted an alternative approach after the War with which they converted their industries into globally competitive enterprises. They adopted Total Quality Management wherein changes are made by teams at many levels in an enterprise, even workers on the shopfloor, who by using systems thinking, analyze and eliminate root causes of poor quality.

The World Bank report points out that "FSSAI realized that it would need to go beyond the traditional standard setting and regulatory-only approaches. It used a mix of regulatory, enabling, and capacity-building approaches, going beyond traditional safety regulatory mechanisms in an effort to tackle the informal economy."

5. Systems improvement is a process of societal learning

The World Bank makes an important observation: "Eat Right India initiatives have evolved over time, reflecting feedback from stakeholders and testing on the ground". It was not designed by a group of experts and consultants who passed on the blue-print to an implementing agency, which is the conventional approach for complex projects. Systems transformation requires many stakeholders to change their own parts of the system while others are changing theirs. They must learn together. The role of the nodal agency is to stimulate a process of systematic learning of new ideas and acquisition of new capabilities across the system.

6. Learning at a deeper level while doing

All 'vocational' skills, including skills for making and implementing policies, are best learned while doing. Therefore, action must be aided by reflection in a quest for learning how to make improvements. For transformational change, learning must be at two levels: at the level of the task in hand—such as improvement in food safety or education; as well as at a deeper level for improving the underlying approach to policy making and implementation.

"Modernizing and innovating regulatory approaches and systems remains a key focus for Eat Right India", the World Bank notes. The hope is that insights from Eat Right India, into how regulatory and systems approaches should be changed, may enable much faster systems improvements in other areas.

(Published by The Hindu BusinessLine in September 2020)

11

Engineering a Governance System

Governments in developed as well as emerging economies are struggling to define an optimal regulatory structure for the financial sector. With too little regulation, the sector becomes unstable, destabilizing the entire economy. With too much regulation, or the wrong regulation, innovation is stifled. Governments are also confronted with a conceptual challenge regarding industrial policy. Industrial planning in the Soviet Union and in India prior to the 1980s killed entrepreneurship. However, free markets with no industrial policy, the theory the US espoused and which became the dominant paradigm of economic policymaking around the world since the 1990s, except in countries such as China, Korea, and arguably Germany too, has not delivered results either.

Now India needs an industrial policy to grow its manufacturing sector to create jobs and reduce its current account deficit. Even the US is developing an industrial policy for the same reasons, to create more jobs and balance its trade. Within the broader scope of industrial policy also lies the vexatious issue of pharmaceuticals that must be addressed in India and in the US too, viz, how to reduce prices of medicines without bureaucratic controls that will destroy incentives for innovation and investment in the industry.

It is safe to say that neither leave it to the market, nor top-down planning and control are the solutions. Insights into systems' architecture can provide governments new concepts for managing complex financial and industrial systems. Broadly, complex systems may be divided into three classes. One is engineered systems. These are systems designed by man, following scientific disciplines, to produce desired outcomes. Machines are the most common manifestation of this class of systems. So are top-down planning systems that control inputs and outputs. However, as all students of engineering learn, engineered systems are subject to the second law of thermodynamics. This law says that the entropy within a system (roughly translatable as confusion within) will inevitably increase over time. Therefore, the capability of an engineered system will reduce over time. The operation of the law is evident in our experience.

Machines must be periodically repaired and renovated by engineers to maintain their levels of performance. And we also know from experience that while planned economies may start vigorously, they lose their abilities over time. Moreover, physical scientists can explain, with mathematical models, that an increase in entropy is inevitable in engineered systems.

The second class of systems is chaotic systems. These are formed by the interactions of millions of independent particles or free agents. The concept of a universally free market composed of free agents without any governmental regulation, that liberal market extremists espouse, has the structure of a chaotic system. Chaotic systems can produce surprising outcomes. The example of a butterfly flapping its wings in Brazil that causes storms in Hong Kong is often cited to illustrate this characteristic of chaotic systems. The near collapse of the global financial system, stemming from problems in the housing loan market in the US, could be another example.

Mathematicians and physical scientists are studying the mechanisms by which the consequences of local events transmit across large system to understand the structures of chaotic systems.

The third class of systems is complex self-adaptive systems. Insights into these have come from a collaborative, interdisciplinary exploration of systems by economists, physical scientists, evolutionary biologists, computer systems experts and others interested in the behaviour of complex systems. These systems display characteristics that neither engineered systems nor chaotic systems have. They increase their capabilities over time unlike engineered systems, and they do this with some underlying logic unlike random chaotic systems.

The most obvious illustrations of such systems are in nature where capabilities of species evolve through competition. Thus, over time, more evolved species develop. Contrary to the second law of thermodynamics, natural systems follow a law of evolutionary biology that says that complex systems will increase their capability over time. The competition in nature does not destroy the whole system. There is some higher order, or some deeper structures—depending on whether one believes in God or is an atheist—that regulates this competition so that the commons on which all depend are maintained. On these commons the competitive game plays out evolving better capabilities in the system over time.

Complex self-adaptive systems sit on the edge between engineered systems and chaotic systems. They neither sink into stasis like engineered systems nor are they an unformed, potentially chaotic mass. They have an underlying architecture that gives them the capability to evolve from lesser order to higher order. Systems' science is bringing together experts, who generally live within the conceptually gated communities of their own disciplines, to understand the whole system rather than defend their intellectual turfs. They are discovering the architectural principles that give complex, self adaptive systems their unique capabilities. Among these principles are: permeable boundaries, minimal critical rules, requisite variety and sufficient redundancy in the system.

Policymakers need a new theory to manage the dynamics of national and international economies. They shun planning and controls. And they no longer want an unregulated economy. A new paradigm they are adopting is the regulation of competition. To tune up regulatory regimes, they could be well guided by emerging insights into the architecture of complex self-adaptive systems.

(Published by Mint in April 2013)

12

Keep Older People Engaged, Don't Isolate Them

The most vulnerable persons during the COVID pandemic are the elderly. If infected, their odds of survival are the lowest. When shut away to save them from infection, they are likely to suffer from neglect — from lack of care for other ailments, and loneliness. The pandemic has highlighted humanity's dilemma of what to do with older people.

Globally, the population aged 65 and over is growing faster than other age groups. Life spans are increasing with better healthcare, nutrition and sanitation. In 2018, for the first time in history, people aged 65 or above outnumbered children. Children are our future, no doubt. However, the changing shape of populations threatens to bankrupt economies. How will fewer young people provide for the care of larger numbers of older persons if the latter no longer contribute to communities?

When the president of Zanzibar received me as the Chairman of HelpAge International in 2017, he posed his dilemma to me. The rights of older people are enshrined in Zanzibar's constitution. It directs the government to set aside money to maintain a good home for older people. He wanted me to see the well-equipped home the government ran. The problem was it was under-used because older people would rather stay with their families.

Later, the minister for social development and the president of the Older Persons' Association explained the President's dilemma. Both of them were grandparents who enjoyed being with their grandchildren, and their families also liked having them around. Grandparents kept an eye on the house and the children when the parents went to work. The arrangement was good for the economy, and for society too, they felt.

I asked what help they wanted from HelpAge International. The minister asked could we convince international aid agencies that their solution was the best one for older people in Zanzibar, and not keep driving the government to set aside more money for facilities to put away older people?

"No place like home" is the heading of the Economist's account of what the pandemic has revealed. Across the rich world, nearly half of all deaths from COVID-19 have happened in care and nursing homes, even though less than 1 per cent of people live in them. Countries with fewer care homes have had fewer COVID-19 deaths, all else being equal.

Older people want to add more life to their years, not more years to their life. As well as exposing fragile business models, the pandemic has highlighted the tension between keeping old people safe and keeping them well. "People should be the boss of their own lives. It is better to live in a house than a warehouse," says Bill Thomas, the American geriatrician who founded the Green House movement for the care of older persons.

All things must be considered before prescribing strong medicines. Indeed, this is why we are so careful about testing new medicines for COVID-19 before releasing them for public use. The pandemic has revealed many factors that contribute to human well-being. Lockdowns — a strong medicine to prevent COVID-19 deaths — have harmed human well-being in many ways, by other medical problems that could not be attended to and even by starvation in poorer countries due to disruptions of the economy. In India, as elsewhere, attention is focused every day on counting the deaths caused by COVID-19. The other tragedies, though not counted, are visible in heart-rending images of migrants struggling to find succour, and people denied healthcare for other diseases.

What we have learned from the pandemic is that local systems solutions, developed and implemented by communities, are necessary to solve complex problems. Communities understand their needs and their capabilities better than experts who are distant from them. Collaboration on the ground has enabled many communities to prevent the spread of the pandemic, as well as taken care of other needs of their members. In India, Kerala, with its systems of local, collaborative action, seems to have done much better than other states. Internationally, countries with strong local systems have done better.

Vietnam seems to have survived the pandemic better than most countries. One reason is the strength of the OPA (Older Persons' Associations) movement which the government has supported for many years. OPAs operate in all districts of the country. They are adding younger members and transforming themselves into Inter-Generational Self-Help Groups. They take responsibility for the most vulnerable people in their communities — most of whom are older people. They also work with local officials to improve local services and infrastructure for the benefit of the whole community. They are "nodes" in networks of actors who know what is required and who can, working together, improve services for everyone. The older members of these groups are proving to be valuable assets for the community. Moreover, because they are active and they feel valued, they add more good life to their remaining years.

Older people have an invaluable role to play in our collective future. We must keep older people engaged, not shut them out to protect their bodies from the virus. Unfortunately, the generic medicine of "physical distancing" to fight the pandemic has been branded as "social distancing". We need "social cohesion", not "social distancing", in communities, and in humanity as a whole, to fight this pandemic and also improve human well-being.

(Published by The Indian Express in August 2020)

B. INDIA

1

My Vision for India

My vision of India is an Inclusive, and Entrepreneurial, Democracy.

My vision is a Deep, and Inclusive, democracy.

We have the largest electoral democracy in the world. But we do not have the deepest, nor most inclusive, democracy.

An elected government is a Government Of the People. It is also expected to be For the People and therefore must be accountable to the People always.

But deep democracy is more than that. It is Government By the People too.

A democracy where citizenship is not merely the right to vote members of assemblies.

But a democracy in which citizenship is also the active management by people of their own affairs in their communities and local bodies.

Not an election time democracy, but a deliberative democracy in which citizenship is the right to understand the rules, and to shape the rules by which citizens govern themselves.

My vision of India is an Inclusive Economy.

Real Inclusion in the economy is not obtained by Handouts and Redistribution. It is achieved by inclusion in opportunities for all citizens to contribute to the creation of growth.

Therefore my vision is a country of Businesses For the People, By the People, and Of the People too.

Businesses must meet the needs of people. Especially those at the bottom of the economic pyramid. Therefore, for inclusion, we need innovations to provide affordable and accessible goods and services. Not just luxury goods for those at the top in which there is a lot of profit no doubt.

More public health services, not five star hospitals. More schools for the poor, not ivy league universities.

There is a business opportunity for profit at the bottom of the pyramid that many entrepreneurs are recognizing. Their Businesses produce For the People. But this does not address the root cause of poverty.

People are poor, and cannot afford to pay much, because they do not have incomes,

They need jobs and incomes to lift themselves out of poverty. Therefore they must be engaged in the processes of producing goods and services for themselves and others. And therefore we need innovations in production models that provide more jobs, so that Business is By the People too.

Less investment of scarce capital in automation. More engagement of human beings in enterprises, because India has the greatest abundance of human beings on Earth.

Employees in enterprises owned by others have incomes, but they do not share in the creation of wealth, the fruits of which go entirely to the owners. Most of whom care only for the growth of their own wealth, and not the condition of those who work to create it for them.

For a fuller inclusion in the benefits of growth, we need more enterprises in which the producers and workers share the wealth creation too. This requires innovations in enterprise design and governance models to shape Businesses which are Of the People too, by being owned by the producers.

In my vision of India, India, which is a country of over a billion democrats, will also be a country of hundreds of millions of entrepreneurs.

Indeed this was Mahatma Gandhi's vision. His charkha was a symbol. In his vision for India, all people would be producers of goods and services that the community and the market need.

They would be earners and also owners of their enterprises, even if tiny.

Also, in his vision, local communities, in villages and towns, would govern themselves, and not be governed from capital cities.

Another piece of my vision for India has become imperative today. It is a vision of the country Gurudev Tagore prayed for.

"A country not broken into fragments by narrow domestic walls".

My fellow Indians, let us be less divisive and more cooperative. Let us respect the differences in our ethnicities, our histories, and our religions.

In my vision of beautiful, diverse, incredible India, no mind will be without fear and every head will be held high, whether covered by a turban, a fez, shaved bare, or covered in a burqa if that be the individual's choice.

My fellow Indians, let us strive together towards a heaven of freedom: a country in which every citizen has all three freedoms: political, social, and economic freedom.

We have a long way to go to meet with our collective tryst with destiny to which we awoke at the midnight hour on 15th August 1947, 73 years ago, when I was just 4 years old.

We have a long way to go. As a nation we have miles to go before we sleep.

In my vision, the country will be transformed by hundreds of millions of young Indians, with a renewed ambition to create the country of our collective aspiration.

They will be the billion and more democrats who respect each other.

As well as the hundreds of millions of entrepreneurs in all walks of life.

Older generations must hand over the baton to another generation of younger Indians.

May you be "fireflies" (lovely jugnus). Each lit up with your own light from within.

And may you all rise together, and we with you, to turn the shadows into light for everyone in India.

Jai Hind!

(Blogpost 15th August 2020)

2

Fast Forward India: The People Make the Difference

SCENARIOS FOR THE FUTURE OF INDIA

An invitation to make a difference

(This document was the outcome of a process of learning together in 1999/2000 amongst many diverse citizens of India from many walks of life and many parts of the country who were concerned about the future of India unless we could find a better way for the progress of the country. I had designed and facilitated their process using the methods of generative scenario planning.)

The Problem

Many thinking and caring people in our country are concerned about where the country is headed. There is frustration with the slow progress in growing our country's economy, and in improving the lot of the poor people of our country. Many experts, Indian as well as foreign, have proposed solutions to accelerate change. There has been progress, no doubt. But it is insufficient and it is slow. 50 years after our Independence, we have 36% people below the poverty line[1], and 44% of our adult population is illiterate. And many countries that were poorer than us are now much further ahead. On the Human Development Index[2], we rank 128 among 174 countries, behind Sri Lanka, China, Mexico, and South Africa. Similarly, on the

---

1 Source: India Economic Survey 1999-2000
2 Human Development Index measures average achievement in basic human development in one simple composite index. It is based on 3 indicators – longevity, educational attainment, and standard of living.

Growth Competitiveness Index[3], we rank 49 among 59 countries, once again behind the above-mentioned countries.

We are a large country, with a lot of diversity. There are so many divisions within the country: many political parties, regions, religions, economic strata, etc. We are very proud of the fact that we are the world's largest democracy. The democratic process requires that different interests must be considered. However, the way the process is playing out in India is getting messier with the various groups acting blatantly in their self-interest. The parliamentary process, by which the many interests have to be finally reconciled, seems now to be anything but a good and reasonable process in our country. Often it is chaotic.

The acceleration of change in the country will require aligned action by many groups across the country: civic society, government, business, and political parties. Our problem is that when we go one step forward, we invariably have to go half a step back because of protests from those who are adversely affected. Hence the continuing concern amongst investors: will India carry on with its process of reforms swiftly?

There are already many forums for discussion and debate amongst the many groups who must be consulted. These include the parliamentary process, as mentioned earlier. There are also many formal and informal meetings outside the parliamentary process, such as meetings sponsored by industry associations between business people and government. Nevertheless the alignment and action is insufficient. Hence the frustration.

Solving India's Endemic Problems

Many complex, systemic, problems have to be solved to accelerate desired change in India. The inadequacy of the education system is one. The poor quality of the physical infrastructure is another. Chronic, and deteriorating power and water supply is yet another. All such complex problems require many people from different institutions, and with different perspectives,

---

[3] Growth Competitiveness Index measures the factors that contribute to future growth of an economy, in order to explain why some countries their prosperity faster than others.

to work together. However they are not working together effectively. Which is why these problems have become endemic.

Fortunately many people have now begun to come forward to address parts of these complex problems, including education, realising that Government cannot solve them. These include corporations, NGOs, individuals, as well as motivated Government officials. This is a welcome development but can lead to complications that need to be managed.

The complications arise from two sources. One is the incomplete understanding by those who want to do good, of the whole system and the interactions of the various forces within it. The other is the egos of the various people who need to interact to understand and resolve the problem. In the story of the four blind men and the elephant, each sees the whole in terms of the part he knows best. The knowledge of all four has to be combined to understand the whole. And they better do this before they rush to action based on their narrow perceptions to avoid causing damage or being hurt. What if the man who thought the trunk was a tree, took an axe to it to chop it, or tried to climb it? Returning to education, the problem cannot be solved merely by changing the content, nor by merely providing computers to the schools. The whole must be understood by combining the knowledge of the experts of the various parts. Only then can their actions contribute to an effective solution to the problem affecting them, and many more Indians.

The other problem, of competing ambitions and egos is often more difficult to deal with. But it is not insolvable. It has been found that if people can share a vision of the whole of which they would feel proud to be a part, and see how their actions would contribute to the whole, they are more willing to collaborate. If they can also see how their individual or collective actions could prevent their desired vision from emerging and devise governance systems to prevent inadvertent or deliberate break-downs, they have a better chance of succeeding.

A Fresh National Conversation

We need a supplemental process in which the various groups can come together in a different spirit. For which we recommend a process that has been found to be very powerful to create deep conversations and learning amongst people who are part of one large system, but who have tremendous competition among themselves and perhaps very different values. And who can, by acting in their own self-interest, inadvertently damage the whole of which they are a part.

The process is Generative Scenario Thinking. It has been used with good effect in many complicated situations. For example, it was used in early 1990s in South Africa, when the differences between the various races and political parties could have blown the country apart.

Generative Scenario Planning emerged from a combination of two disciplines of management. One is Scenario Thinking (or Scenario Planning) which Royal Dutch Shell and other corporations began to use in 1970s and 80s to understand the complex phenomena that impacted their business. For Shell, the price of oil is an important variable that can cause big swings in the company's performance. The price of oil is determined by interplay of many variables, some political, some economic and some technological and is pretty much outside the control of Shell. The other discipline is Vision Alignment, the essence of which is to align the aspirations of key players in a system.

Using a combination of both these disciplines, the Generative Scenario Thinking process focuses the parties involved on *what might happen*, as well as on what each of them would *like to happen*. However, it is *not* a process of negotiation, wherein one must identify the positions and interests of the parties and find a way to narrow and reconcile them. Thus Generative Scenario Thinking avoids the differences among the participants, and concentrates on the domain that all the participants have in common – which in the South African situation was the future of South Africa. The participants, in the process did not have to agree, in the first stage, on a concrete solution to the country's problems: they only arrived at a consensus on some aspects of how South Africa "worked", on the complex nature of the crisis, and on some possible outcomes of the current conditions. At the same time, the recognition of a shared aspiration for the future stability of South Africa greatly facilitated the parallel processes of negotiation which also had to take place since the 'system' included people with divergent interests.

The approach, techniques and tools of Generative Scenario Thinking have been applied in recent times to national level problems in many countries including Japan and Canada. It has also been used in many diverse situations such as improving the delivery of public education in the USA, developing business strategies in the oil industry, to setting environmental policy.

An Invitation

Some months back, a group of people gathered in Delhi and used the approach of Generative Scenario Thinking to address the questions of 'Whither India' and 'What are the drivers to accelerate the change we all desire?' The group included senior government officers, business people, social workers, academicians, and politicians. They also involved students, women from rural areas, and homeless street children. Everyone joined in their individual capacity because they personally cared, and not as representatives of their institutions. Inputs from this diverse group, together with research into relevant subjects, through the structured process of Generative Scenario Thinking, produced four scenarios of what India could very well be in the next 10-15 years. The drivers of the desired change were analysed, and examples of how they could operate were found. The Confederation of Indian Industry (CII) provided the platform for this process. Arun Maira, now the Chairman of The Boston Consulting Group in India, facilitated the process.

This document presents the summary of the groups' output, which is four scenarios and five 'driving forces'. These are offered as seeds for thoughtful conversation, and a stimulus for action by people who would care to make a difference.

These scenarios have been shared in many forums across the country recently. Some people have turned away from further engagement because they fear all this is hopeless idealism. However many others have come forward with new hope to make a difference. And some have already begun to stimulate action in their own spheres with resources they can influence.

Indians who care to make a difference need a different *approach* to thinking and working on today's problems. If many caring Indians *act together*, putting their weight behind the drivers that can really change the country, we will get the India we want. As Robert Kennedy said in a speech in South Africa:

> "It is from numberless diverse acts of courage and belief that the human story is shaped. Each time a man stands up for an idea or acts to improve the lot of others or strikes out against injustice, he sends forth a tiny ripple of hope. And crossing each other from a million different centers of energy and daring those ripples build a current that can sweep the mightiest walls of oppression and resistance."

What can you do to make a difference?

Scenarios for India 2010

WHAT WILL INDIA BE LIKE IN 2010?
Four Scenarios

- India 2010 — Buffaloes Wallowing
- India 2010 — Wolves Prowling
- INDIA 2000
- India 2010 — Fireflies Arising
- India 2010 — Birds Scrambling

The next section depicts these scenarios as metaphors and descriptions of what life would be like for people in India in these four different scenarios.

India: Scenario I

Buffaloes Wallowing

The buffaloes continue to wallow in the swamp. It is time to move on. Who can goad them? The herdsboy yells to them that they will go hungry if they do not make a move. One or two attempt to get out of the water. But they are surrounded by others. So they give up.

India Scenario I: Description

Buffaloes Wallowing

The problems of the enormous country are very difficult to put one's mind and arms around. Macro-economic solutions are easy to prescribe but very difficult to implement. So many different interests have to be reconciled.

The balancing of state and central budgets is obviously desirable. Excessive employment in State enterprises must be cut back. But it is so difficult to reduce expenditures and employment significantly when some groups will have to do with less here and now for the sake of benefit to the whole society in the future. Shock treatments that will hurt large numbers of people cannot work in a strong democracy.

No one seems to be able to do anything to accelerate desired change in the country. Every worthwhile solution seems to require many people to act together. Whether it is in education, or rural development, or industrial growth. Government, businesses, and communities, all have a role to play. In living rooms and conference halls, people describe the grand solutions. And they also are frustrated by their inability to implement them.

Some point fingers at others as the root cause of the problem—at ineffective governments, at apathetic communities, at businesses that cannot compete internationally. Some others understand the weaknesses as well as possibilities in the system and just get on with making the most of themselves. Either way, there is little aligned action in effect to produce the required change in the condition of the whole system.

People throw garbage out of their own homes, and complain about unclean Indian cities. People ask for favors, and complain about the corruption of Indian organisations. Power workers suffer when the transport workers go on strike. Transport workers suffer when power workers go on strike. People keep hurting each other to gain something for themselves.

Stories have emerged of communities here and there in the country that have changed their own conditions by people acting together in responsible ways. Water has been harvested. Roads have been constructed. Some banks and companies have facilitated improvement in some areas. The stories add to the list of interesting things people can talk about together. However, the talk does not lead to much action.

There is no crisis. Life is unlikely to get much worse. And people do not know how on earth it will get much better in their life times. May be it will happen by itself or it won't. Chalta hai!

India: Scenario II

Wolves Prowling

The land has become a wild jungle. Bands of wolves roam. Small animals, and even big animals, live in fear of these marauding bands. Who can control them? Only the well muscled and armed tiger is safe.

India Scenario II: Description

Wolves Prowling

Populist politics has bankrupted several States. The infrastructure in these states has crumbled.

Corruption has become rife, inspite of some heroic efforts by individuals and organisations to fight it.

The desperation and anger of the poor in the face of the growing wealth of the rich has led to increase in crime, violence, and rioting.

Sectarian differences have been fanned for political gain in many parts of the country. In the North, East, and South, separatist movements have gained strength and terrorism is on the increase.

The problems in neighboring countries are adding fuel to the domestic fires.

Everyone has to look after themselves. Those with money and muscle are better off, but are not secure. The rich have found ways to send their money out of the country. The local stock markets have collapsed.

The Government is incapable to stop the rot.

India: Scenario III

Birds Scrambling

Grain is strewn in the courtyard for the birds. They have been waiting for the food. They scramble for it. The pigeons flap their wings and push the smaller sparrows aside. The sparrows hop around the pigeons hoping they will get to eat also. The pigeons peck away at the grain with no concern for the sparrows. A peacock arrives and the pigeons also retreat. The food is over. The peacock and even the pigeons fly off contentedly. The sparrows have gone hungry. May be tomorrow they may have a chance.

India Scenario III: Description

Birds Scrambling

India is rapidly integrating with the global economy. Imports and exports have been deregulated. Foreign companies are investing in many sectors. Foreign money and foreign goods are flowing in. Several Indian companies, unable to face large foreign competitors have sold out to them.

Central and State government have yielded, at last, to economic imperatives to balance their budgets. Public sector companies have been restructured and privatised. Government subsidies have been cut back. Prices of electricity, water, and fuel have been raised to cover their real costs. Ports and airports are run by private companies and operate efficiently. Foreign and Indian investors are taking advantage of new opportunities for business that are opening up rapidly in India. Change in India at last is lauded in the Western business press.

Many Indian businessmen, taking due advantage of the new opportunities, become very wealthy. Middle class people have more choice in the goods, services and entertainment they can buy. There is a zestful sense of progress in the air, in business offices and in middle and upper class homes.

Business organisations have cut back on non-productive expenditures. They cannot afford to provide housing, education, and other services. Corporate budgets for community services are under pressure. The focus on productivity improvement in business and in government has also resulted in lay-offs.

Governments and businesses cannot afford to provide for the poor. The poor are waiting, impatiently, for the trickle-down of benefits to them. Many scramble from the rural areas to the towns and cities to seek peripheral jobs. Slums grow. The contrast between those who can now have more and those who hope to have someday somehow is even more immediate.

Meanwhile the poor in the rural areas continue to multiply. The problem is the size of the population in India, say the economists and business people. The are too many to be provided for through subsidies. The are too uneducated to be engaged in modern processes of production. And they are too poor to be a market for the modern products and services of the companies coming from outside India and the similar products of the Indian companies that are competing to survive against these foreign companies.

India: Scenario IV

Fireflies Arising

At first, a few bright lights emerged from the darkness. Then many more. Soon the countryside is alight with dancing fireflies. It is wondrous to see how such tiny beings can transform the night. Where did they come from?

India Scenario IV: Description

Fireflies Arising

The country is transformed. All over the country, communities have taken charge of themselves. With assistance from government and non-government organisations, villages have harvested water. Sanitation has been improved.

Innovations in the telecommunications infrastructure by many Indian entrepreneurs have provided almost every village with access to the Internet. Farmers track the prices of their produce, and also the availability of seeds and fertilisers to find the best times and markets to buy and sell. They bank via the Internet. As do many small enterprises in villages.

Many business leaders from the cities have discovered the reliability of women, related perhaps to their sense of responsibility for their children and families. They have put women at the center of innovative approaches to engage local communities with new business opportunities. Now women play a very large role in the new rural economy. This has brought them into contact with new ideas.

Innovations in the delivery of education have enabled children and adults to acquire knowledge and skills relevant to their needs. The Internet has contributed to this. So have schemes to use the time of retired people and part-timers. Besides, creative use of space available in the communities has reduced the expenditure required to build new schools. Education is accelerating real improvement in the conditions of the poorer parts of the country. And people are making much of the improvement themselves.

Enlightened corporations have been an important catalyst for accelerating these changes in the lives of people. Leading corporations have created new markets for their services and products by including the poorer people in both rural and urban areas in their schemes for growth of their businesses. Thereby they have also brought knowledge, incomes, and hope to many poorer sections of society.

The change in the role of the Government in development has been critical also. Many government officers have been good enablers of change. They have supported the communities by removing obstacles and facilitating access to the requisite resources by the communities.

In many parts of the country, the attitude of people towards responsibility for producing the desired changes is very heartening. People are working together—communities, businesses, government and non-government agencies—to produce change that all want. While in some few parts of the country the pace of change has yet to accelerate, we are no longer despondent. We know how it can be done. It is being done. We have the fruits.

Accelerating Desired Change

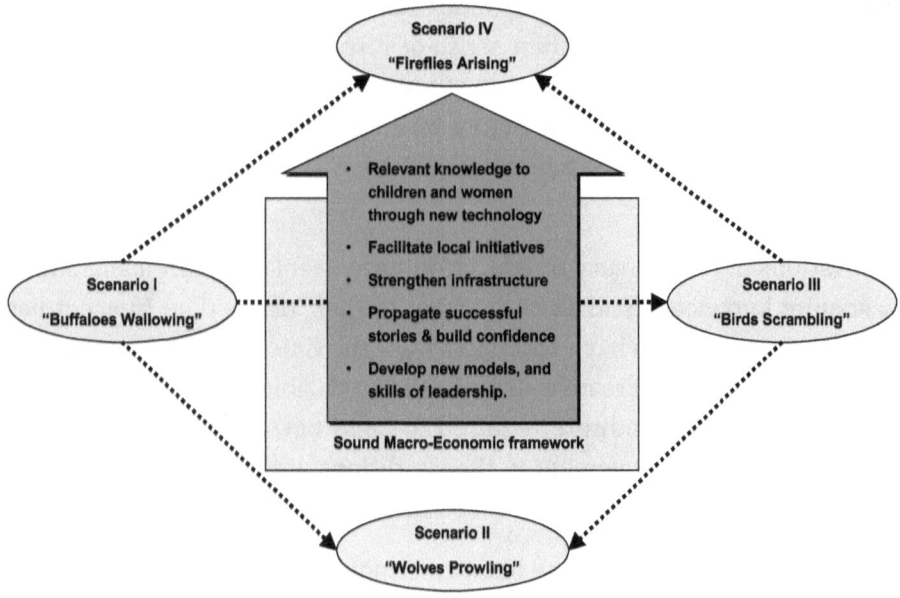

India: Many Million Fireflies Now

(Scenarios of India prepared by CII/WEF in 2005)

Will India make it? The famous BRICS Report says that India will be the world's third largest economy, after China and the US, by 2050—far ahead of even Japan. But we cannot be sure.

We should not forget that 20 years back analysts had projected that Japan would be zooming into the 21st century which would be the Japanese century. But ten years later, Japan stumbled. And who remembers that in 1975 the Soviet Union was the second largest economy in the world, closely rivaling the USA? Nevertheless, 15 years later, it had disintegrated. Analysts' predictions often turn out to be very wrong. Therefore how sure can we be what India will be like even 15 years hence, let alone in 2050?

Just now, China's growth is tantalizing, perhaps even frightening the world. The Chinese have their act together. Whereas progress in India, which is going through an era of coalition governments, is slower. According to many Indians who envy the remarkable improvements in China's cities and its infrastructure, we suffer from the drag of democratic processes. Many economists opine that in poor countries economic growth should precede democracy. However, India cannot go back on its history. Though it is poor, it is a democracy and its people, even its poorest, will not give up their democratic rights. Therefore Indians have no option but to improve the way their democracy functions by tackling two, inter-related questions:

- What is the process by which a large, diverse, and democratic country can accelerate its development?
- What is the appropriate model of leaders for this process?

A few years back, a large and diverse group of people in India applied themselves to these very questions. They were concerned that, while India seemed to have escaped the Hindu rate of growth that had dogged it until the 1980s, and had begun to change and grow faster since the 1990s, the improvement was not fast enough to eradicate the country's enormous problems, such as poverty, failing social services, and poor infrastructure. They used a process called 'generative scenario thinking' in which the underlying forces within a complex situation are analyzed—not only the 'facts' that are visible above the surface. Thus, by understanding the interplay of underlying forces, insight is obtained into what is likely to emerge in the future. The diverse group in India, including economists, senior government officials, journalists, artists, businessmen, teachers, students, political leaders, and others combined their varied perspectives and constructed a systemic view of the Indian reality that they could not have seen from their own, narrow, perspectives.

With these insights, four scenarios emerged of the forces of change shaping India's future. Since a picture can say more than a thousand words, evocative images from India's own Panchtantra folk tales were selected to convey the essence of these four models of change and leadership. Recently when the World Economic Forum wanted to examine the future of India on behalf of its international members, it also used the process of scenario thinking and it built its scenarios with these insights.

Let me describe the scenarios of how India may change over the next 20 years and what the outcomes may be.

'Atakta Bharat': Buffaloes Wallowing

The first scenario of leadership and change is called 'Buffaloes Wallowing'. This is a familiar sight in the Indian countryside: buffaloes cooling themselves in a pond. It is difficult for any of them to move because they are surrounded by others. In this scenario, many experts and bureaucrats, and such people in their 'high-up' positions are expected to determine the policies and changes required and to bring them about. However, they cannot all agree on what should be done. When one proposes, others oppose, and nothing much happens. (We loosely call such people in high positions 'leaders' regardless of how ineffective they are.) Meanwhile, the people in the country wait for progress, especially the young people who will need jobs when they grow up. Imagine a little boy on the side of the pond. That is the future of India, waiting for the so-called leaders to agree and move. The WEF called this scenario 'Atakta Bharat', which means India (Bharat) intermittently stalling as it progresses, hampered by a lack of consensus amongst the various political groups.

'Bollyworld': Peacocks Strutting; Wolves Prowling

The second scenario of leadership and change, called 'Peacocks Strutting; Birds Scrambling' is the story of the free market and trickle down—get the government out of the way and leave it to business. In this story, a woman scatters grain in her yard for the little sparrows to eat. Some pigeons arrive and push aside the sparrows. Then a peacock arrives in their midst and even the pigeons move aside. All the birds look with awe at the peacock and admire its finery and its size. The sparrows hope that after the peacock has eaten, there will be something left for them, if not today, then the next day. The so-called 'leaders' of society that are admired in this model are the wealthy, like those whose expensive clothes and revels are displayed in the electronic and print media.

It is this scenario the Indian Prime Minister drew attention to at the annual meeting of the Confederation of Indian Industry in May this year. He worried about the reaction of the have-nots to ostentatious displays of wealth which they felt may be too far beyond their reach.

The third scenario of leadership and change, 'Tigers Growling; Wolves Prowling', is about the uses and abuses of concentrated power. This scenario often arises as a reaction to the peacocks strutting amidst scrambling birds. Sometimes, frustrated by perceived injustices and the inability of democratic processes to address them, people will support dictatorial leaders who claim to take up their cause. In this scenario of the law of the jungle, the tiger that cannot be challenged by other animals gets his way. However, around him, wolves prey on helpless smaller animals. But the tiger doesn't care. As Lord Acton said, 'power corrupts and absolute power corrupts absolutely'. Like the wolves in the jungle, the powerful leaders' family and friends feed on the little people who live in fear of them.

India is presently experiencing the simultaneous advance of both these scenarios—Peacocks Strutting with Birds Scrambling, and Tigers Growling with Wolves Prowling. The WEF called this combo-scenario 'Bollyworld', after 'Bollywood'—the popular name of India's vibrant film industry. Like a Bollywood movie, this scenario combines glamour and fun with tragedy and violence. And like a Bollywood movie, which must come to an end, perhaps this scenario is not sustainable.

'Pahale India': Fireflies Arising

The fourth scenario is different in a fundamental way. Unlike the others, it puts the onus for leadership and for making change happen deeper into the system and not only on leaders at the top—whether buffaloes, peacocks, or tigers. India is a diverse, democratic and complex system.

The theory of 'complex self-adaptive systems' says that dynamic systems with great diversity (like India) cannot be 'controlled' from a single center. Change in India will be brought about by many hundreds of thousands of people who take the initiative in local centers of action, rather than waiting for an all-powerful (and hopefully benign) leader to emerge at the center.

This scenario is called 'Fireflies Arising'. The picture is a dark, hot, summer night in the Indian countryside. Little fireflies arise out of the surrounding darkness. Their numbers increase. Soon the night is aglitter with myriad bright lights. Fireflies are living lights, carrying their own light. The fireflies in this scenario are the leaders, whoever they may be and wherever they are, who take the first steps towards what they deeply care about in ways that others wish to follow. In this scenario, many Indians in many walks of life take responsibility for making change in their lives and in the world around them. The WEF called this scenario 'Pahale India'—India First.

India has many fireflies arising already, in many forms, and their numbers are multiplying. Millions of women in self-help groups, the increasing number of social entrepreneurs, the proliferation of small businesses, exemplar CSR by some corporations, and even government officials who are producing change through innovations, are all examples.

Sir Vidya Naipaul's first book on India, in 1964, was titled, *"An Area of Darkness"*. His next, in 1976, which pointed out the deadening effect of government on India's progress, was called, *"India: A Wounded Civilization"*. His third, in 1990, was *"India: A Million Mutinies Now."* Perhaps the scenario of India now emerging is **"India: Many Million Fireflies Now."**

All three scenarios of India are based on evidence and hence are plausible. In fact, one can see elements of all of them in the country at this time. But which is the best option for India? CEOs and economists want numbers, not pictures. Therefore the WEF commissioned two econometric modelers, one in the UK and one in India, to run its three scenarios in their computers and determine what would be the rate of growth in India's GDP and reduction of poverty in each of them. They confirmed that Pahale India with Fireflies Arising produces the highest and most sustainable growth, exceeding 10% even, and the fastest reduction in poverty. Bollyworld could also produce a burst of similar high growth but it would not be sustained because tensions within Indian society would create impediments.

India's growth rate has begun to nudge towards the 10% rate that both 'Pahale India' and 'Bollyworld' promise. India's development path is at a juncture now. If Indians want to make Pahale India their preferred way to the future, they must identify the forces that bring it about and strengthen those forces.

Analysis by the group that developed the scenarios of India revealed that, in addition to a sound macro-economic framework, five forces that should be made much stronger to produce the scenario of Pahale India with Fireflies Arising are:

- Provide relevant education to children and women through new technology
- Facilitate local initiatives
- Strengthen infrastructure
- Develop new models and skills of leadership
- Propagate successful stories and build confidence

That is the way to generate the many million fireflies that will transform India, giving it light all over. The essence of this approach is to release the energy at the bottom of the pyramid, rather than create large, top-down programs. Many examples of such fireflies are already visible in India. The challenge is to multiply them, and 'scale up' their benefits without creating a large scale organization for this purpose because that would kill the spirit of local initiatives, and would produce more wallowing buffaloes than fireflies. Instead, the increasing scale required must be obtained by enabling the many local initiatives, in regions, states, and localities, to link with each other, as well as learn from each other.

Several government policies and programs are now enabling this to happen. The unified VAT tax system and changes in agricultural marketing laws are facilitating smoother commerce across state boundaries. India's telecommunications infrastructure has leaped ahead and mobile connections across the country are now even easier to make than in the USA. In a massive national program, roads are being built to connect all of India's villages, in addition to a grid of modern highways across the country.

In addition, for more Indians, men and women, to have access to opportunities when they have the will, they must have access to finance on reasonable terms, and, above all, to education.

Many schemes, both private and government, are directed towards meeting the financial needs of people at the 'bottom of the pyramid' in innovative ways—micro-lending to women's self-help groups is one of them. Education reform, to enable equal access to education, to provide a good education from primary to higher levels, and to modernize and expand vocational education, is India's crying need today. Another area for reform is healthcare. India's huge pool of young people, which is expected to provide the demographic dividend to India's economy in the next few decades, must be healthy, educated, and employable. Otherwise such large numbers of young people could be a huge burden rather than an asset. Therefore education and healthcare are now the focus of much attention in government, the private sector, and civil society also. It is very likely that innovative solutions will emerge from the intensive interactions amongst these sectors.

Finally, it is India's destiny to develop a new model combining democracy and markets that will create growth with equity, and thereby take a huge and diverse nation from poverty to prosperity, and many millions from serfdom to opportunity, on a scale and at a speed never achieved before in human history. India seems to have found signs indicating the path it must follow, a path not taken before.

4

Letter to The Prime Minister, Dr. Manmohan Singh, Published in The Hindu, in May 2009

Dr. Manmohan Singh, the time has come for you, your government, and India, to make a seminal contribution to the world. You have the mind and the heart to do this.

BusinessWeek asked the question, on its cover page, "Wall Street: How Corrupt Is It?" The Economist had a special report on "Capitalism and its Troubles". Both journals raised their concerns seven years ago, in May 2002. Though the warning bells were rung then, the party became even wilder, and greed on Wall Street has contributed to a global economic crisis that has shaken up the capitalist system. The Economist had worried then that its warnings would not be heeded because 'the will to reform may be lacking especially if the world economy continues to recover'. Which it did. Now it is in the doldrums because the reforms were not made.

Dr. Singh, now that you do not need the support of the Left parties, Indian business leaders are clamoring for you to implement their reform agenda. These are the same reforms—to reduce government involvement and open up more sectors for investment—that they had asked from your previous government. A hint that you may do so makes the stock market soar. However the philosophy from which these reforms spring—to increase corporate investments and profits, and GDP—is from the same school of economics that was driving economic policies in countries in the West that are now suffering its consequences. The medicine those countries are now taking to cure their economies is what their economists had so far described as poison, viz. government involvement in corporate affairs. Now 70% of US banks (in terms of pre-crisis capitalization) have some form of government investment; the largest US insurance company is in the government's ICU; and the largest US auto company is being supervised by government.

Business must be free from national boundaries so that the global economy can grow again. Business must also be free from excessive government control so that it can innovate and expand. But business cannot be free from responsibility for the larger good of society. Dr. Singh, throughout the go-go years just passed, you have quietly and courageously reminded our business leaders of the responsibility that must be theirs along with their freedom. In 2006, you addressed CII's Annual Meeting and asked our business leaders to voluntarily take up affirmative action. There was a hue and cry from them.. They thought the father of economic reforms had betrayed them. At CII's 2007 Annual Meeting, you outlined a ten-point plan for business' responsibility to society. There was more consternation. And in 2008's Annual Meeting of CII, you laid out an agenda for inclusive growth of the country and invited business to come along.

President Obama has told American business leaders that they are being held accountable by the people, that economic growth in America must be more inclusive, and that a new philosophy is required for business management. That philosophy cannot be 'first profits and then philanthropy'—a philosophy that Jack Welch, an icon of the era passing by, repeats in an article this month. Because it is how the profits are made that must change. There has to be more inclusion of community interests in business, and more care of the environment. Business' performance must not be judged only by the profits it makes and the wealth it creates for shareholders. Its management must voluntarily hold itself accountable for environmental and societal measures, else regulations will be imposed.

Economists and business leaders struggle to reconcile the requirements for efficiency and equity. They do not have the models and tools for this. Michael Spence along with other Nobel Laureates on the Commission on Growth and Development end their thoughtful report on ways to increase GDP of countries with a deep concern for increasing inequality. They say it is a problem begging for an urgent solution. Because size and efficiency, which are simpler to quantify, have become central to economic models, whereas equity is a fuzzier concept.

Therefore economists need new concepts and tools. Those who speak for business and efficiency must come together with those who speak for inclusion and equity. They do not because they dismiss each other as 'Right' and 'Left' and do not want to be even seen in each others' company.

"Reforms must be pro-market, not pro-business, and governments should keep their distance from business and their bosses". If the Indian Left, or Mamata Banerjee, had said this the thought would be dismissed as stale ideology. But when it comes from The Economist, the staunch defender of capitalism, in a cover story on 'Capitalism and Democracy' (in June 2003), even Indian business leaders and right-leaning economists must take note. The Economist says, "In democracies, governments have to be the arbitrators, the counterweights to powerful private groups. But if they allow, or even encourage, companies and wealthy individuals to manipulate them, they risk stretching public faith in democracy to breaking point."

Dr. Singh, India needs a social and political consensus about the philosophy that will take it to its tryst with destiny. Reform policies must follow from this. Healthy democracies require not just elections. They also require platforms for dialogues to reconcile differences. The democrats of ancient Greece conducted such debates civilly and in public view in city plazas. In India, the Emperors Ashoka and Akbar created councils for dialogue between people with different beliefs. Institutions for public dialogue in the Indian democratic state are not functioning at this time.

Parliament now meets less and less, and when it does, its proceedings degenerate into shouting matches and walk-outs. Discussions in our media are set up as 'big fights' for entertainment to attract advertisers. Political differences are being settled on the streets.

Fortunately, some seeds for a new dialogue have been sown during your previous government. One is the Indian Institute of Corporate Affairs promoted by the Ministry of Corporate Affairs. It is as an autonomous institution to bring together thought-leaders from business, government, civil society, and academia to evolve new frameworks and ideas for economics and business, and for the reform agenda India needs, and perhaps the world too. In the tradition of Ashoka and Akbar, such dialogues to open-mindedly seek consensus on a new philosophy must be high on your priorities and have your active encouragement.

5

Flotilla Advancing

Scenarios:
Shaping India's Future

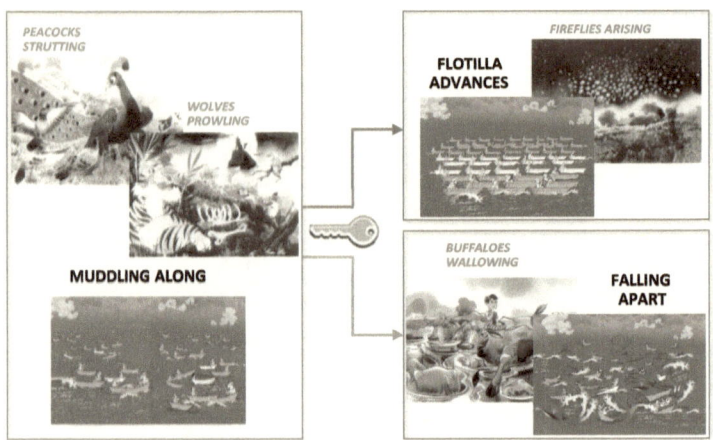

October 2012

Scenarios, Turning Points, Directions

Two questions are being asked with increasing frequency both in India and around the world. Is our pattern of economic growth sustainable? And, is our pattern of growth fair? It is clear that a new approach is required for human development and societal progress. If the prevalent "theories-in-use" to define progress, manage development, and govern societies continue, the risks to the environment and to social harmony are very large.

The 12th Plan and Scenarios for India

Planning in India was required to be a participative process, with inputs from the people. However, each five-year plan seemed to drift further away from the language and concerns of people into the realms of economic numbers and financial budgets. Therefore, it has become necessary to adjust the method of planning, to connect planners more strongly with people.

The figure below illustrates the various tiers of planning. Most of the time, discussion is "above" the waterline—allocations and design of schemes. What is more important is "below" the waterline.

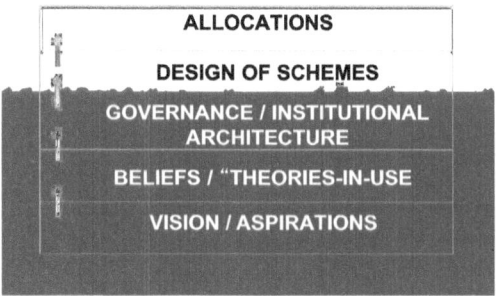

Navigating the ship versus fitting out the cabins

The purpose of "scenario thinking" is to project "what if". What if we do not change our underlying theories-in-use about progress and governance? Alternatively, what if we begin to adopt alternative theories. Scenarios are projections of plausible outcomes of alternative courses of action. They can help us choose the strategies that produce the outcomes we want. Scenarios enable dialogues, which in turn lead to agreements. Therefore, a team of Indians with diverse backgrounds has developed scenarios to facilitate new, collaborative conversations, amongst citizens and policy-makers, about India's future. The Prime Minister (and Chairman of the Planning Commission), Dr. Manmohan Singh, while asking the Planning Commission to reform itself, has directed it to become a "systems reforms commission" and an "essay in persuasion". Scenarios, explain the reforms to the system—the "theories-in-use" and the "policy-matrix"—required to produce faster, more rapidly inclusive, and more sustainable growth. However, people must understand the fundamental shifts in policy required and support them, and press the political system for change. Thus, scenario planning is a complement to the traditional planning process, and represents an innovation made in the 12th Plan.

The System Model

The relationship between the fundamental forces that emerges from our systems analysis is presented in the diagram below.

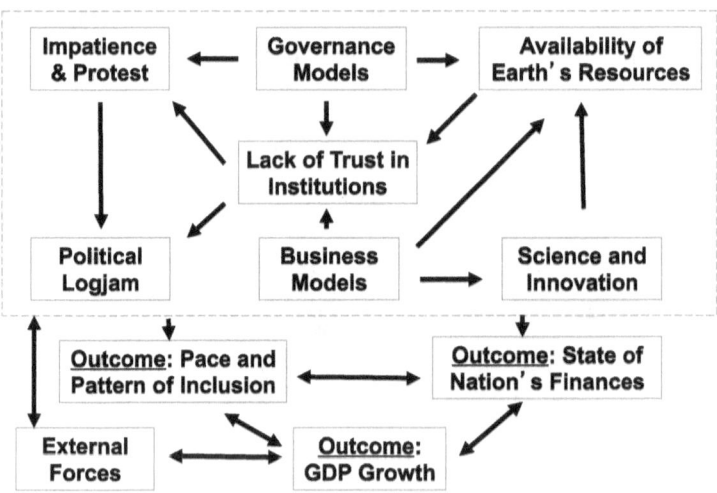

Figure: Root Causes and Leverage Points

The analysis locates the leverage points: the forces that affect the condition of all others. These lie in the design of institutions and are seen in the middle of the diagram. The architecture of governance impacts trust in institutions of government and large business. Business models have a direct effect on science and innovations, which in turn impact the sustainability of the earth's resources. Lack of trust in institutions increases impatience in society, leading to a political logjam, which makes reforms that the system needs more difficult.

The condition of the system, and its ability to reform itself will determine the pace and pattern of inclusion in growth. It will also affect the state of the nation's finances. Therefore, predictions of GDP growth rates must be related to the condition of the system and the social, political, and institutional forces within it, which are often treated as exogenous to economic growth models. Finally, the condition of external factors that impact India's progress is not easy to forecast. Therefore, the most important question for the country's policy-makers must be: what strategy will ensure that the country will be best placed regardless of these external uncertainties? Not surprisingly, India will be most secure in times of uncertainty if it is internally cohesive and strong. Therefore when the world around is changing, the Plan for India must concentrate even more on institutional reforms within.

Three Forks in the Road to the Future

Many of the strong forces that will shape our future, like the demographics of India and the spread of communications with new technologies, are "givens". However, other forces that will strongly shape our future are not necessarily givens. The future shape of the system—the quality of the inclusion as well as the financial condition of the economy—will depend on the choices we make.

Like an X-ray, the systems' analysis shows a deeper pattern. When we make certain choices, many other forces that depend on them will also go accordingly. And, when they go another way, another "scenario" altogether can emerge. It is not surprising that the three fundamental forces located by the systems' analysis that can shape India's future are about approaches to development and governance

A. The approach we take to "Inclusion": the What and the How of inclusion?

A principal challenge for economists and policy makers all over the world has become how to achieve "Inclusion" along with economic growth. Two contending approaches are evident. One emphasizes "redistribution": taking from those who have more, and giving to those who do not have enough. The other approach emphasizes creating more access to opportunities, so that the less well-off can increase their incomes faster and also contribute to growing the pie. At one extreme, the emphasis is mostly on "handouts". At the other extreme is a very determined effort to generate more opportunities for livelihoods and to provide all sections of society with access. Scenarios can project the consequences, of choosing one course rather than the other.

B. The approach we take to "Governance": will we strengthen local, community based, and collaborative governance rapidly?

When systems seem to be "not in control", the instinct is to centralize. However, if the reasons for the results not coming faster are that the diversity in the system is very large and therefore solutions must be locally adapted, and that there is not a capable center, then it may be best to strengthen local governance rather than try to impose central control. The need to break across the silos and create convergence has been recognized.

At one extreme, the way most things are run is, in effect, "central" and "silo-ed". At the other, local rural and urban governments are effectively in charge of their affairs with vigorous participation of local citizens. In a devolved structure with power closer to where results are required, and with different parts of the system working collaboratively, adaptation and learning are faster too.

C. The "theory-in-use" towards energy and environmental solutions (as well as enterprises): big projects, or more community-based solutions and enterprises?

Local and smaller solutions can create more ownership and responsibility for the use of resources and also ensure more equity in distribution of benefits. The argument against this theory is that scale is required for more efficiency. Innovations in networked enterprise designs can enable the benefits of both, local ownership, as well as the benefit of scale where required. On one end, big is good is the dominant paradigm. At the other end, only small is beautiful.

Each scenario is a description of the system it describes (the country in this case) if forces play out, or are caused to play out, in one way rather than another. Internal consistency requires that implausible combinations of directions of the forces are not considered. The India scenarios described in this document are constructed around the leverage points in the more fundamental forces explained above. They are derived from an analysis of all the critical forces identified in the scenario process. Thus, the scenarios are comprehensive, and internally consistent, descriptions of different States of the country's future.

Three scenarios of India's future

The system analysis reveals three scenarios of India. They can be described under the headings of Insufficient Action (*Muddling Along*), Policy Logjam (*Falling Apart*), and Strong, Inclusive Growth (*The Flotilla Advances*). These scenarios result from three different configurations of the three "theories-in-use" outlined previously.

Scenario 1: Insufficient Action *(Muddling Along)*

This is the scenario of India where the system is crying for reform, and some reforms are initiated. However, these are piecemeal, do not address core governance issues, and therefore are not effective. Centralized government systems struggle with demands for decentralization. Small enterprises are sought to be encouraged, but the agenda of big business dominates. The policy conflict between subsidies and financial stability of the economy remains unresolved.

The picture

The many diverse communities that compose our nation (class, caste, region, etc.) can be imagined to be sailing in ships in a flotilla on a sea that is often rough. The sea they are navigating through is the external global and national environment, and the increasing stress on the earth's resources. The flotilla would like to move faster but is slowed down because the ships are unable to keep together.

The sea has become more turbulent. The ships are not talking often enough for all to collectively decide on their direction. At the same time, the engines and navigation systems of the ships (their institutional capabilities and governance models) have not been updated to suit the more turbulent environment so they are not able to travel faster and to coordinate quickly with the flagship.

Often, one ship moves ahead faster than the others, but it has to wait impatiently for the laggards to catch up. Sometimes a storm separates the individual ships and it is difficult to bring them back into the flotilla and on course. Other countries' flotillas in contrast seem to stay closer together and are able to maintain a higher average speed.

The explanation

As the government engages in piecemeal reforms, some positive feedback loops are created within the system. A shift away from subsidies, allows for some more education and employment opportunities. Hopes rise, but since the progress is not fast enough, impatience increases the pressure to ease poverty with subsidies and large handouts.

A lack of politically difficult reforms hampers progress. A centralized government, inherently inefficient at allocating resources compared with localized government, impedes outcomes of centralized schemes. Innovation is stifled by a lack of autonomy and precious natural resources are wasted. This increases lack of trust in institutions, resulting in continuing protests and political logjam.

Reforms are made but many are stalled or diluted. The economy grows but hardly achieves its full potential: insufficient social and political cohesion remains a threatening source of instability.

Scenario 2: Policy Logjam *(Falling Apart)*

This scenario emerges from India remaining stuck in a centralized governance system whose theory-in-use is to exert control in the face of demands for devolution, by centralized mega-schemes and projects, and by "redistribution" of wealth through a system of "handouts" and subsidies. The impatience and political logjam that result put India under severe stress, with several factions threatening to dissociate themselves from the political union.

The picture

A flotilla of ships is trying to sail together, but ships keep colliding with each other. The ships do not communicate enough. Consequently, ships often sail off in different directions. The flagship is spending too much time just getting the flotilla back together, leaving little time to coordinate future directions.

> *Only in a calm sea does the flotilla move faster. When the sea becomes stormy, and the ships often cannot even see each other, much less the horizon that they are to sail towards, they fall apart. Moreover, since the ships don't have an updated chart of the seas they are sailing in, they sometimes hit uncharted rocks. Thus some ships are left behind while others move on.*

> *These setbacks are disheartening the flotilla's crew. They hear of the rapid advance of other flotillas. They also hear the frequent confused signals between the ships in their own flotilla. This makes them even slower in responding to any misfortune that strikes their ship—consequently, making it harder to recover.*

The explanation

In a system where hardly any institutional reforms are made, a vicious cycle emerges which results in the political logjam becoming so severe that government can barely function.

Extremism infects more areas of the country. Stand-offs between central government institutions and between the center and the States become rigid. Governments try to win popularity with increasing hand-outs. Civil society protest movements take up non-negotiable stances. The political logjam becomes worse. Hand-outs strain governments' finances. Investments slacken. Employment does not grow as rapidly as the potential workforce, so India's demographic changes become a ticking time bomb. Handouts do not incentivize innovation and entrepreneurship, but instead create dependency. A cash-strapped government is unable to achieve its goal of poverty alleviation through subsidies.

Needless to say, both the pace and pattern of growth and inclusion are far off target. Any belated attempts at reform are now stymied by a central government with limited financial or political capital to deploy.

Scenario 3: Strong, Inclusive Growth *(The Flotilla Advances)*

This is the future of India with a federal governance system in which the wheels begin to mesh more smoothly, local governance institutions and small enterprises are nurtured and grow effectively. Livelihood opportunities, along with community based solutions and enterprises for addressing environmental issues, are seen to be sprouting.

The picture

> *The flotilla is well coordinated with better navigation and communication systems between all the ships. It has created a system to arrive at a consensus about the direction the flotilla must take. The ships are manned by inventive crews, empowered to try new ways to speed up their ships. With good communications between the ships, new ideas from one ship are transmitted quickly to others. Consequently, all ships are improving their abilities to navigate and sail faster.*
>
> *The flagship has ensured that all ships have a map, know the route to take, and have good instruments to guide themselves, and coordinate with others. When ships temporarily lose contact with others in a storm, they are able to return to the path and rejoin the flotilla. Their confidence in their ability to progress and in their captain motivates the crews to go about their work satisfied that they are individually and collectively moving ahead.*

The explanation

The government vigorously takes up necessary reforms in government processes and regulatory systems, along with pending economic reforms.

States have flexibility to devise local solutions while also linking the assistance to agendas for governance reforms. In inclusion, governance, and sustainability, a self- sustaining positive cycle emerges. People are engaged, not alienated.

"Networked enterprises" such as farmer cooperatives, clusters of small and large enterprises, create a wider spread of opportunities for citizens to earn better livelihoods. Faster growth of economic activities and employment opportunities increases government revenues and reduces the demand for handouts. A challenge in this model of distributed authority is the "scaling up" of good solutions across the country. However, by learning from each other, every part of the system is enabled to improve faster, and the overall outcome for the country is scaled up faster.

Participation and more innovations make the whole system internally stronger and provide greater protection from external shocks.

Thus decentralized governance and solutions along with a focus on opportunity-based inclusion produces more sustainable strength— socially and economically.

India at a Turning Point: Which Scenario Will Emerge?

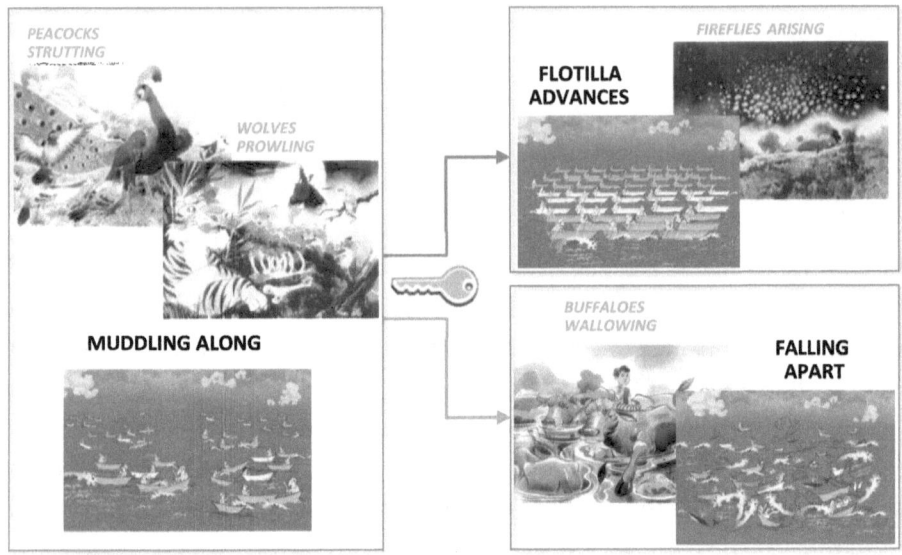

 India is currently described as Muddling Along. If we now focus on implementing the overdue governance reforms, we can expect a speeding up of the India flotilla's progress and cohesion. If we do not implement governance and institutional reforms very soon, we can expect a further falling apart of the system and the India growth story.

Planners cannot create a spirit of shared vision in citizens: they can only provide paths and plans for realization of the vision. At most, they may provide a seed to start conversations about a shared vision for India's future. These scenarios are spurs for conversations about the shape of India, the type of country we want to be, and the models of governance we must develop.

The scenarios, along with the system analysis of forces, and elements of an emerging vision, provide starting points for a new conversation between the Planning Commission and stakeholders, and also amongst citizens. There is no guarantee that this process will result in a consensus. But, it is certain that, in the absence of a good dialogue about these issues, a consensus is even less likely!

The questions are: What is the character of the country we want, and how will we build it together.

NOTE: This is a condensed version of the original Scenarios document released by the Planning Commission on July 10th, 2012. The original full-length document can be accessed at http://goo.gl/aWiVN

APPENDIX

EXTRACT OF PM'S STATEMENT AT THE FULL PLANNING COMMISSIONMEETING

September 15th,
2012
http://goo.gl/emQBo

"The central message of the Plan is that we can achieve our objective provided we put in place policies that will take care of our weaknesses. The Plan for the first time introduces alternative scenarios.

Scenario one is called "Strong Inclusive growth". It presents what is possible if the policy actions outlined in the Plan are substantially implemented. One can expect a number of virtuous cycles to start operating, leading to positive results on both growth and inclusion. This is the scenario we should aim at.

Scenario two is called "insufficient action". It describes a state of partial action with weak implementation. The virtuous cycles that reinforce growth in Scenario I, will not kick in, and growth can easily slow down to 6 to 6.5 percent. Inclusiveness will also suffer. This is where we will end up if we make only half-hearted efforts and slip in implementation. It is my sincere hope that we do not do so.

Scenario three is called "policy logjam". It reflects a situation where for one reason or another, most of the policies needed to achieve Scenario 1 are not taken. If this continues for any length of time, vicious cycles begin to set in and growth could easily collapse to about 5 percent per annum, with very poor outcomes on inclusion. I urge everyone interested in the country's future to understand fully the implications of this scenario. They will quickly come to an agreement that the people of India deserve better than this.

I believe we can make Scenario one possible. It will take courage and some risks but it should be our endeavour to ensure that it materialises. The country deserves no less."

6

India: A Slow Learning Country?

The Indian state has many challenges. A major one is to ensure that economic growth creates jobs much faster than it has so far. A large, youthful population can provide a demographic dividend to the economy. It can also create huge societal and political problems if there are not enough jobs. Another looming challenge is to improve the ability of the state to perform its functions and provide services to citizens more efficiently.

No doubt India has progressed a lot over the past 60 years, more in the last 20 with the acceleration of economic growth. However, it must progress much faster on improvement of human development indicators and creation of jobs. Its manufacturing sector, which must be a principal source for more jobs, has been a laggard. Manufacturing accounts for only 15% of India's gross domestic product (GDP), whereas China's, at over 30% (of a much larger economy), has been the principal driver of employment and growth.

Citizens' mounting frustration with the inefficiency and corruption in services that the state must assure—security, health, education, urban utilities, and transport infrastructure—was a principal factor in the dramatic defeat of the United Progressive Alliance government in recent elections. Statistics of how much poverty has reduced, how many more children are in school, and how much more power is being generated than before, did not satisfy them. They need more and want more. Citizens were also put off by the arrogance and corruption of leaders of political and government institutions. India must reform institutions and produce results much faster. A related issue is the performance of the Planning Commission and its relevance in the 21st century.

"Creating a Learning Society: A New Approach to Growth, Development, and Social Progress", a new book by Joseph Stiglitz and Bruce Greenwald provides a new lens through which one can diagnose the capability of the Indian state and progress of the economy. The perspective of learning as the primary driver of progress also suggests a fresh way to consider the role of the Planning Commission in a 21st century economy.

Stiglitz and Greenwald's argument can be summarised in three points. One, they say that economics has become too narrow in its attempt to be precise. Economic models leave out the dynamic sides of societies—institutional capabilities and innovation, which are their unquantifiable but primary sources of development. The second point is that the essence of social development and economic growth is a process of learning. Countries learn to do what they could not do before. And if they learn faster than others, they develop faster and grow faster too. Thus Japan, then Taiwan, Korea, Singapore, and now China have swept ahead of others.

Their third point is that the process of industrialization has been the principal cause of growth of economies and living standards. It is when societies learnt to make things they could not make before, and to develop more efficient processes for making these new things, that growth took off exponentially. Thus, incomes and living standards have improved much more in the last 200 years, by industrialization, than they had in the previous two thousand years.

Several other economists—Dani Rodrik, Ricardo Hausmann and Ha Joon-Chang, to name a few—have recently argued countries grew their industrial sectors by learning faster than their competitors at the time. This explains Japan's, Korea's and China's progress in recent times, and Germany's, the UK's, and US's before that. Ergo, a country's industrial policy must principally be a process to stimulate institutional learning—in firms and state institutions and their interactions; rather than allocation of resources and permissions, which was the orientation of India's industrial planners until the 1980s; or even picking winners, which is controversial.

Stiglitz says that a clue to how countries learn can be found in how industrial firms learn. He points to the extensive literature on the subject which economists and policymakers should turn to. It is heartening to note that, in India's 12th Five-Year plan, the paradigm of faster learning as the essence of industrial policy, is explicitly applied at last. Unfortunately, it has not been picked up by the government so far. It must, for India to grow its manufacturing sector much faster and create the many millions of jobs required in the next few years.

Several developing countries are progressing faster than India on many fronts. India and China are large countries. Both were very poor 60 years ago. India has no doubt progressed, but China has progressed much faster, not just in economic growth but also in health and education where improvements were faster than in India, even before China's GDP growth took off.

The Indian state is a slow learner. It must learn to learn faster, and implement faster, to accelerate development and growth. Therefore, rather than assisting the government to allocate funds, which has been its principal role so far, the Planning Commission's principal role must be catalytic. It must have within it world-class expertise in enterprise learning processes and institutional design to assist the union and state governments to learn and implement their plans and processes faster.

(Published by Mint in August 2014)

The Great Scramble of Indians to Board India's Economic Bus

We need an economic model that goes beyond conventional paradigms to address the ground realities of our common people

The covid-19 pandemic has highlighted the structural weaknesses of India's economic model. As gross domestic product (GDP) was growing, the bus was moving. The few people inside it were comfortable. But when the bus suddenly braked, the huddled people crammed on its roof and clinging to its sides (because there was little space inside) were thrown off onto the road. The moral tragedy was that those inside the bus did not know that so many people were travelling along so precariously. They were out of their sight, and even out of mind.

Old debates among Indian economists have begun again—the debates of 1990, and even those of the 1970s and the 1950s. Global trade or domestic industries? Large scale or small enterprises? Industry or agriculture? Urban or rural development? The most contentious debate among economists is one that has started again, recently, on global versus local. Those economists who had pushed policymakers to make a bold break from the past and engage with the world after 1991 now fear the return of an old, pre-1991 kind of nationalism, which emphasised self-reliance, small industries and village enterprises. India must remain "vocal for global", they urge.

The defence of free global trade, in the midst of so much evidence that we cannot carry on the way we are, appears weak. Even economists admit that they are searching for a "new, more sustainable normal" since the financial crisis of 2008-09, which they failed to anticipate. They know their science is not adequate. Therefore, they must learn and change—for the academic purpose of making more accurate predictions, and also in response to an ethical imperative to devise policies that would include those who have tenuously been hanging on to the country's bus of GDP growth.

A bedrock principle of trade economics is the theory of competitive advantage. If all nations stick only to what they do best, and buy from others what the latter can do better, the global economy will be larger. Because there will be no waste of resources by those who are less efficient than others. The theory does not explain how the citizens of all nations will get a fair share of the global pie. In fact, according to the theory of rational self-interest—another bedrock principle of mainstream economics—those who have a competitive advantage (and the power that comes with it) will fix the rules of the game to preserve their edge.

Simplistic trade theory ignores that competitive advantages are neither God-given nor permanent. Nations can develop capabilities that they do not have and compete successfully. This is how nations have always developed their economies: Japan, South Korea and Taiwan after World War II; Germany and the US before it; and China recently. All of them have been accused of being "protectionist" at some stage, like the US was by its European rivals in the 19th century.

Good sports coaches do not throw trainees into the ring against champions right away. They spend energy outside the ring to build their trainees' capabilities. Aspirants enter competitions progressively, challenging tougher contestants as they improve. India's policymakers must devote much more attention to the building of India's internal capabilities if Indians are to benefit from participation in global trade. Several economists—Dani Rodrik, Ricardo Hausmann, Ha Joon-Chang, and others—who have been advocating the need for sound industrial policies, to create more competitive enterprises and employment within countries, have so far been outside the mainstream because their ideas run counter to the dominant school of free trade economics. Enterprises learn, and policymakers must continue to learn too, they have argued, so as to create a "learning society" that can learn faster than all its potential competitors can. Joseph Stiglitz and Bruce Greenwald expanded this idea in 2014 in their book, Creating a Learning Society. Disciplines of "organizational learning" have been developed and applied outside the discipline of economics for over half a century.

Economists do not need to reinvent the wheel. They could humbly learn from others.

Economists everywhere are beginning to admit that they must go back to school to invent a new economics. India needs a new economic model. It should be neither the model that existed before 1991 when growth was slow, nor the model since then, which has not delivered inclusive growth. Our economists must move on from the debate of whether pre-1990s socialism was better for India's masses or the post-1990s adoption of capitalism. Trade economists, labour economists, industrial economists and all other types of economists must step outside their specializations, and see reality from many perspectives together. Moreover, they must listen to "non-economists" with other insights.

The shape of growth matters, not just its size. The pandemic has woken up economists. "Vocal for global" without much "vocal for local" will not create a resilient and just economy. Policymakers and economists at the steering of the bus must listen to the voices of the millions who have been holding on to it for their dear lives and livelihoods, while those within were provided the comfort of cushioned seats and safety belts.

For India to grow inclusively and sustainably, new forums are required urgently, within formal institutions and outside, for participative development of solutions that take into account the real concerns of the country's population. Economists who formulate policies must engage people on the ground.

We need a new development model. This requires expertise, no doubt. But experts need the people of India to acquaint them with reality and also suggest practical solutions.

(Published by Mint in July 2020)

8

The Poor State of the Indian State

Two new books reveal stark weaknesses of the Indian state in serving India's poorer citizens. The first, *Locking Down the Poor: The Pandemic and India's Moral Centre* by Harsh Mander, records the plight of millions who lost incomes and shelter, and food and medical care too, in a harsh lockdown to create a sanitised cordon for better-off Indians during the pandemic. "Every system is perfectly designed to produce the results it is presently producing", said Donella Meadows, a doyen of systems thinking. The second, *Despite the State: Why India Lets Its People Down and How They Cope* by M. Rajshekhar, is an incisive examination of the systems of the Indian state before the lockdown. These books explain how the weakness of the Indian state to care for its poorer citizens is not a failure of the present National Democratic Alliance government only, nor of the previous United Progressive Alliance government. The weakness is systemic.

The Pillars Needed

Strong states, according to political and social historians, are founded on three pillars. They are built with support from the people; they have a strong administrative machinery to provide stability and deliver public services, and they have the managerial ability to shape and implement change.

Strong support of the people is essential. Mere election by a majority is not sufficient. Historically, as Francis Fukuyama points out in *The Origins of Political Order*, builders of strong states have bound people around a shared identity: ethnic, racial, or religious; Aryan, Han Chinese, Japanese, Muslim, Catholic Christian. The peoples' identity is not formed by legal constitutions. Strong leaders who unite people around their shared identity are even given liberty by the people to change constitutional structures because they trust their leaders do it for the sake of citizens. Thus, dictators emerge loved by the people.

Confirming this thesis, Michael Cook points out, in *Ancient Religions, Modern Politics*, that builders of the Indian state have a difficult problem. It is hard to unite Indians around a shared ethnic or religious identity because, in addition to the diversity among India's races and religions, there are entrenched caste divisions even within the Hindu religion of the majority. If Indians must be united to support a strong state, it must be around a modern, inclusive idea of India, as the Constitution imagined. The present ruling dispensation, while trying to force a majoritarian identity, is dividing Indians and weakening the state.

Indian Bureaucracy's Role

Fukuyama and other historians have highlighted the role that professional civil services have played in the formation of strong states, in Han China, the Ottoman empire, France, and Japan. India inherited the 'iron frame' of civil services from Britain. It was designed to provide stability and compliance with rules: it was not equipped to shape change, the third requirement of a good developmental state. Therefore, there are demands for its reform. Even the Prime Minister has complained that bureaucrats seem not to care for the country's progress as much as entrepreneurs do.

Simultaneous management of both change and stability is necessary for the evolution of good states and societies. Unmanaged change can cause chaos, while too little change entrenches the established system. This was the essence of the 'great debate' in the 18th century between Edmund Burke, the leader of the conservative movement in Britain, and Thomas Paine, a thought leader of the French and American revolutions. It was also the 'birth of Right and Left' in politics, according to Yuval Levin in his eponymous book, *The Great Debate*.

The great debate, about stability versus change for good governance, evolved into new arguments in the 20th century: capitalism versus socialism; and markets versus governments. By the end of the century, capitalism and markets were positioned in the public imagination as the prime movers of economic growth, and socialists and governments as retarders of progress. Capitalists took on the mantle of 'wealth creators', relegating governments to the role of 'redistributors'. A popular slogan that wealth must be created before it can be redistributed leads to the conclusion that there should be less government when countries are poor, and more freedom for large, private, wealth creators. Moreover, with the logic that governments are stodgy, even public services such as health and education are handed over to private enterprises.

The logic of economics is not the same as the logic of society. Mancur Olson, author of *Power and Prosperity: Outgrowing Communist and Capitalist Dictatorships*, says that privatisation of government fits with 'efforts of economists to extend their model of rational, utility-maximizing behavior into the political realm and to see politics as nothing more than an extension of economics'. The ideology of private is good and public is bad requires that public servants should think like private sector managers — committed to growing the pie — and not think like socialists concerned about the condition of the people who are waiting for wealth to trickle down to them. To assist them, consultants from the private sector are brought inside government to help the state run more like a business corporation.

Where the Focus Should Be

Private corporations are not states designed for citizens. CEOs are not elected by employees, and they have the authority to hire and fire workers. Whereas leaders (even unelected ones) of states cannot lay off citizens to trim populations to fit the size of economies. The state must perform primarily for its poorest citizens for economic growth to be equitable and sustainable, and not for investors in corporations. Leaders of states must ensure that all citizens have opportunities to work and earn. They must also ensure that all citizens, even those who cannot afford it, have good health and education.

The ideology of private rather than public has moral consequences. The purposes of a private enterprise and the state are different. Private sector managers move from one competitor to another, like professional mercenaries, serving the interests of owners of corporations wherever in the world they may be. Whereas public servants, whose mission is to build their nations and states, are expected to devote their lives to the care of citizens in their own countries.

GDP Cannot Be The Scorecard

The pandemic has revealed the chronic inability of the Indian state to take care of its poorest citizens. The scorecard for the nation cannot be its GDP. Economic justice, environmental sustainability, and improvement of the dignity of all citizens must be measured too, and these must improve much faster. The present 'top up the top' model of India's economic growth, with hopes of trickle down, is not delivering these.

India must build a strong and good state. This requires: political leaders who can unite all Indians into one India, whatever their religion, race, or caste; cadres of good public managers to build and run services for all citizens equitably; and business leaders who are not just wealth creators for themselves (distributing some of it in philanthropy), but creators of opportunities, very soon, for millions of Indians to earn and create wealth for themselves too.

Political leaders, administrators, and business leaders must work together, with a shared vision, to build an Indian state that is good for all citizens, especially the poorest. Time is running out.

(Published by The Hindu in February 2021)

9

Listen to the Voices of the Less Powerful

Indian farmers want better prices for their produce. The NDA government has promised to double farmers' incomes. Recently, it pushed ahead with "pro-market" reforms. Farmers in northern states — the richest farmers in India — are against these reforms. They say the reforms will harm, not help, farmers. The government says they are being misled. What is the truth?

The problem of India's agricultural sector, according to economists, is that there are too many people employed in agriculture. Whereas the agriculture sector contributes 17 per cent of India's GDP, it employs 57 per cent of the workforce. The solution, according to economists, is to improve the productivity of Indian agriculture and reduce the numbers employed. For the agriculture sector to become as productive as other sectors of the economy, it should employ only 17 per cent of the workforce — the overall size of which is estimated to be around 500 million. Therefore, approximately 200 million workers must migrate from agriculture to other sectors. However, other sectors, especially manufacturing, are not generating enough employment. Moreover, there too, wages and incomes are fragile. In manufacturing also, the problem is low productivity economists say. They recommend more "Industry 4.0", that is, more technology and automation, to improve productivity. To which sectors then must India's masses migrate to earn decent incomes?

The problems of low prices for farm produce and low wages for workers are political economy problems. The terms of trade are stacked, as they always are in unregulated markets, in favour of the large against the small. The large have more power in "open markets" to obtain prices in their favour. The small have no capital and savings to fall back on. They have to "take it or leave it" and thus their wages and prices are kept low, which are "good deals" for buyers and employers.

Protests against the agricultural reforms whose ostensible objective is to make markets free have come from farmers in the north who have been the greatest beneficiaries of the system that is proposed to be dismantled. They are richer than farmers in other parts of the country who have not had the benefits of government support. These rich farmers are portrayed as selfish people preventing reforms that will help poorer farmers.

The vilification of protestors diverts attention from the core issue, which is that farmers have not been able to improve their incomes in those parts of the country where government intervention has been minimal, and markets have been supposedly free. The guaranteed minimum price applies to only a few crops and covers less than 10 per cent of the overall farm produce. The APMC mandi infrastructure covers less than 17 per cent of the market — there are less than 7,000 mandis, whereas 42,000 are required overall. So, how will further deregulation help them?

Labour unions are also caught in a political trap. The terms of employment are most secure, and wages have risen, in large establishments where unions have been strong. When these unions raise concerns about the security of employment and wages for the 95 per cent plus of India's workers who are not employed in these large establishments, they are painted as representing India's "spoiled" workers and are accused of preventing other workers from benefiting from labour reforms. Labour reforms are necessary, the unions say. They agree with employers that procedures must be simplified, and outdated laws changed. However, they say the reforms must enable workers to learn and earn more, and with greater safety and dignity than the vast majority of Indian workers presently have.

For this, it is essential that workers in all establishments have the right to have their grievances and suggestions heard by their employers. As individual workers they are powerless. Therefore, for the sake of their welfare, and to meet the national objectives of improvement of the well-being and incomes of all citizens, all workers must have the right of association in unions. In the labour reforms underway, it is the dilution of this fundamental right of collective representation that bodes badly for India's workers, and for Indian democracy too.

NITI Aayog's CEO says tough reforms are difficult because India is "too much of a democracy" ('We are too much of a democracy... tough reforms hard: Niti chief's wisdom', IE, December 9).

The concept of democracy should not be reduced to elections and political parties. Democracy is also a process of listening to all stakeholders. The government's dismissal of the concerns of farmers and workers to push through "bold" reforms is not only bad for democracy, it reduces the quality of policies and also makes them harder to implement.

Three fundamental reforms are necessary to make India's growth more just and more inclusive. The first is, policymakers must listen to the less powerful people in markets. Therefore, institutions that represent small people — associations and unions of farmers, informal workers and small enterprises — must be strengthened, not repressed. When reforms are supposedly in their interests, they have a right to be heard.

The second is the formation of cooperatives of producers and workers. By aggregating the small into larger-scale enterprises owned by themselves, not only do the producers have more power in negotiations with their buyers, suppliers, and with government, they are also able to retain a larger part of the value they generate and increase their own incomes and wealth. Government regulations must encourage the formation of strong cooperatives, and improve their ease of doing business.

The third is, market reformers must clean up their ideological lenses and see the reality of where power lies in markets. As Barbara Harriss-White, a scholar of India's agricultural markets once observed, "deregulated imperfect markets may become more, not less, imperfect than regulated imperfect markets."

(Published in the Indian Express in December 2020)

10

The Listening Deficit

"The democratic process cannot be allowed to be subverted through unlawful protests," Prime Narendra Minister Modi tweeted, commenting on the storming of the US Capitol by Donald Trump's supporters. Meanwhile, thousands of farmers are camped in bitterly cold weather around India's capital. They are peacefully protesting amendments to farm laws the government has rammed through without a discussion in the country's elected Parliament. They threaten to carry out a peaceful tractor march in Delhi on the nation's Republic Day if their demands are not conceded by then. These protests in the world's two largest democracies raise questions about the health of the global democratic enterprise.

What is a "lawful" protest? Who determines whether the purpose of the protest is lawful? And which methods of protest are lawful? If such questions should be discussed within a democratically-elected Parliament (or Congress), and if elected institutions do not function, should the people not protest? They must protest, albeit non-violently, in a manner that will make their protest heard as the Indian farmers are, and the protestors in Shaheen Bagh were.

Experts advising the government are prepared for discussions with the farmers provided the discussions are "evidence-based", they say. Which raises more questions. What is evidence required for? What is acceptable as evidence? The experts have their own scientific models about what is important. The farmers have their experience of what matters. Experts want more hard data. Whereas farmers' mistrust of the government's intentions is based on their experience, including the way in which the reforms are being rammed on them. That's not how democracy is supposed to work, they protest.

Liberals everywhere are feeling threatened by the rise of autocratic leaders. Elected leaders may say they work for the people and listen to them. However, the experts who advise them plug people as numbers into their scientific models, even looking down on them as uneducated masses. When leaders rely too heavily on expert advisers for solutions, trust in elected leaders breaks down. Trump rose up on a global wave of citizens' mistrust in the way democratic institutions are functioning. Trump may have fallen, but the wave of illiberalism has not passed. It has risen due to the failure, so far, of two projects to meet citizens' expectations of improvements in the human condition — the project of electoral democracy, and the project of scientific rationality.

The Indian government is being urged by economists and industrialists to implement economic reforms firmly. The people who are the intended beneficiaries are not convinced, as the farmers' are saying. Even experts disagree amongst themselves whether the reforms are the right ones. Indian economists have been very critical in recent years of the Supreme Court's "interference" in the economy, with its decisions in tax matters, etc. It does not have the necessary expertise for economic policies, they say. Caught in the impasse of agriculture reforms, the government now seems inclined to let the Supreme Court decide what should be done. Is this not an admission that the government and the economists who advise it do not have the expertise required for democratic governance?

The expansion of the idea of human rights is the mother force of democracy. Democracy is deepened by the realisation that those who rule always have more power than those they rule over. The nobility over peasants; white people over coloured people; upper castes over lower castes; employers over workers; men over women. The advance of ill-regulated capital across the world in recent years, to promote the ease of doing business rather than ease of living, has given those with more wealth greater power to frame rules than citizens who have no wealth. Democracy must correct this.

The fault-lines in democracy are: Ill-regulated capitalist markets are corroding democracy; experts are misinformed about realities; global elites, who are connected in a global community transcending national borders, are disconnected from common people. They think "global" and believe that thinking "national and local" is going backwards whereas people within countries everywhere, especially those left behind in the global race, want their governments to look inwards to their needs first.

The Edelman Trust Barometer, an annual global survey of citizens' trust in institutions reported, in 2020, that: "A growing sense of inequity is undermining trust in all institutions — government, business, the media, even NGOs." Government, the media, and NGOs are supposed to serve the people. Even businesses realise they must be trusted by the people for their license to operate. They should not have to turn to the government to convince citizens that big corporations are good for the people. Because then the people will believe that the government and corporations are in cahoots to serve corporate interests, and they will lose faith in their own government.

Trust is decreasing because no one is listening to others. The government is not listening to the people, neither are experts. Experts in their specialised silos are not even listening to experts in other silos. Social media is forcing people further into gated communities of "people like us" who are unable, and unwilling, to listen to "people not like us". Democratic governance is breaking down because no one is willing to listen to people they don't understand or agree with.

The fundamental reform India needs (and the world too) is a "no tech" one. It is the process of listening to people who do not seem to think like we do. By listening to other perspectives, we will comprehend the system of which we are all small parts; and economists will improve their science too. Moreover, by listening better to each other we can trust each other, and then we can work together, democratically, to make the world better for everyone.

(Published by the Indian Express in January 2021)

11

Fix the Process of Reforming Policies

The Indian economy is in a slump, and so reforms are an imperative. But the complications of banking sector reforms, the ongoing struggle of labour reforms, and the saga of agricultural reforms have all made clear that India's policymakers are having a hard time pushing ahead with reforms. Arvind Subramanian, former chief economic adviser to the government, says that "restoring dynamism (in the economy) requires improving the 'software' of policymaking itself: the way that policies are formulated, publicly articulated, and implemented." That policies to produce desired outcomes require good processes, not only domain expertise, is vividly clear from the agitation of farmers against the new laws the government is trying to impose on them by side-stepping democratic processes.

The necessity of reforming processes for plans and policy was highlighted by former Prime Minister Manmohan Singh in his second term, when he commissioned an internal review of the Planning Commission. Economic growth, though fast, was neither inclusive nor environmentally sustainable. Several people from industry and civil society said India needed more plans and policies. They recommended that the Planning Commission be changed into an 'implementation commission'.

The celebrated 'first-generation' reforms of the 1990s reduced controls on industry. They applied to a limited set of stakeholders, compared to the more difficult 'second-generation' reforms necessary in land, environment, labour, agriculture and public services. Implementing these democratically is more difficult because they need the participation of a much wider range of stakeholders. The country needs systematic processes to convert contentions among stakeholders into consensus, and confusion in implementation into coordination, so that the intentions of plans and policies are translated into outcomes. India has good economists and domain experts, but needs better processes for making and implementing policies. Manmohan Singh said that the Planning Commission should transform itself from an institution making plans and allocating funds into a "systems reform" commission, and into an "essay (force) of communication".

An international benchmarking exercise was undertaken with the World Bank's assistance to learn how other democratic countries make and implement policies, especially those with good track records of inclusive growth, such as Germany, Japan, Sweden and Korea. The study revealed that the key was systematic involvement of citizens and stakeholders. The principles of good processes were distilled, and best practices studied. These were being put into a package of 'software' for dissemination to states and ministries by the Planning Commission when the government changed.

The Indian state has an unusual capacity for large-scale implementation. It conducts elections on a very large scale, whereby hundreds of millions of voters, even in very remote areas, cast their votes. The administration of the pulse polio vaccine to make India polio free is another example. Wherever 'one size fits all', and a standard procedure must be applied, the Indian state can do it well. However, when variations are required to suit local conditions and behavioural changes are needed, such as in the design of toilet solutions, school education and public health, community participation is essential. Local-system solutions implemented by stakeholder communities are necessary for such systemic problems.

Reforms are even more difficult when fundamental rights and questions of justice are involved, as they are in matters of land, labour, agriculture and the environment. In these domains, policies cannot be designed by 'technical' experts only. Voices of citizens must also be listened to. Stakeholders must be involved early on to get the policy right and gain support in implementation. Moreover, the quality of stakeholder engagement determines the quality of the policy.

Government functionaries claim they consult others extensively. However, most consultations are purely proforma. Representatives of stakeholder groups are invited to meetings, and their attendance noted. In most meetings, they are lectured to and their views briefly noted, which they are assured will be considered. Draft policies are put on websites and comments are invited within a few days. Most citizens are not aware of this. Some do respond, and their responses are counted as 'consultation' even if they are not read by policy formulators. Many stakeholders do not have the technological wherewithal to download and respond to huge files. The numbers of persons supposedly consulted may be impressive, but in effect, there is hardly any consultation.

The principal complaint of Wada Na Todo, the platform created by civil society organizations to give feedback to the erstwhile Planning Commission under the United Progressive Alliance-2 government was that planners and policymakers do not really listen to people. They consider citizens to be uneducated masses who must be explained to (if at all), not listened to. The concerns people express are dismissed as either illogical objections or political obstructions. This is the principal cause of today's impasse over farm reforms.

Constitutions, laws and formal institutions are the hardware of democracy, while processes of dialogue between the government and citizens and among citizens themselves are its software. This software is essential for economic policymaking too. India's software of policymaking is poor, and the software of its democracy is breaking down. The government must fix it. Else, the trust of citizens in its ability to govern well, and democratically, will diminish.

(Published in Mint in January 2021)

12

Recoupling the Economy with Society

The Covid 19 stress test has starkly revealed fundamental flaws in the design of the global economy. Global supply chains collapsed, shutting down entire industries, and throwing millions out of work. In my own country, India, the precariousness of the incomes and lives of people outside the enclaves of rich globe-trotters, who were out of their sight and even out of their minds, could not be hidden any longer, when millions of internal migrant workers spilled out onto roads and highways, to walk to their homes in villages hundreds of kilometers away, seeking food and shelter, which was denied to them by a global system they had come to serve. These were India's used and discarded workers, who had been contributing to the growth of its GDP.

For many years before the pandemic, I was struggling to unlearn ideas of economics and public policy that have dominated the official global discourse, which I was actively participating in, to learn other ideas which I sensed were needed. It was not easy. I found myself challenging not only myself, but also having to challenge my own side in a debate about paradigms.

While everyone was locked in, I was able to connect more easily, surprisingly, with other like-minded people, who for some years have been questioning the prevalent paradigm of economic progress. So far, they had been on the margins of the debates about economics. Now they needed to be heard from. I was inspired by the weeks' long Global Solutions Summit which has just concluded, and the dozens of conversations it enabled amongst thoughtful people around the world, on the urgent need for 'Recoupling the Economy with Society'—its theme.

A Conflict of Paradigms of Growth

Metaphorically speaking, the two sides were: the side of the World Economic Forum gathering on the mountaintop in Davos—the side I was seen to be on; and the side of the World Social Forum gathering on the ground by the sea at Porto Allegro. During the last thirty years, the distance between the two increased further; with the wealth of the people 'up there' soaring higher and higher above the wealth of the people 'down there'.

When I joined India's Planning Commission in 2009, I found the two sides in opposition within the country. On one side were economists and bureaucrats in the Planning Commission (PC), and on the other side were civil society organizations in the National Advisory Council (NAC) (which was sometimes referred to as a 'parallel planning commission'). When the UPA government fell in 2014, and both the NAC and the PC were disbanded too, the debate amongst economists continued publicly. On one side were Professors Jagdish Bhagwati and Arvind Panagariya, both advocates of free trade for growth. On the other were Professors Amartya Sen and Jean Dreze (the latter a prominent member of the NAC), both advocates of human development for growth.

Prof. Panagariya was appointed the head of the new National Institution for Transforming India (NITI Aayog) which replaced the Planning Commission. The new government was urged to step up reforms of the economy. 'Reforms' meant more openness of the Indian economy to international trade. And dilution of labor protection laws to make life easier for business investors. However, the weakness of India's growth model, which had been producing high growth of GDP for some years (and which had enabled India to declare itself as the world's 'fastest growing free market democracy') were becoming evident too. Employment was not growing enough. Which was dangerous for a country with the largest numbers of young people in the world—the source of the expected 'demographic dividend' to India's economic growth. In fact, India had the lowest employment elasticity of growth in the world—that is the numbers of jobs created with each unit of GDP growth.

The 'other side' of the policy debate became emboldened to say that India needed a good Industrial Policy to build domestic industries and create more employment within India, a concept that had almost become taboo with the Washington Consensus. According to this side, what India needed, much more than relaxation of worker protection laws, was universal social security for all citizens. However, they were sneered at by the other side as 'socialists' and 'protectionists' and relics of the past.

When the government was forced to declare a harsh lock-down in March to prevent the spread of the Covid virus, the fragility of India's growth model was revealed. Now the government is scrambling to provide 'social security' to hundreds of millions of workers who have lost their jobs and incomes. And, it is trying to rapidly build domestic industries, and to support small enterprises, who will employ more people in more secure jobs. India's planners are being compelled to shift their priorities, to focus on the small and not the big; on rural villages rather than on urban metropolises; and on people first rather than on investors. Back to fundamentals; back to the roots.

A searching has begun for a new paradigm, to replace the one that was neither resilient nor just which has dominated economic policies for the past thirty years.

Returning to the Future

Sixty years ago, a prescient economist in the UK had predicted that, "the twin evils of unemployment and mass migration" would break out into a pandemic in developing countries unless the paradigm of 'economic development' was changed. He was E.F. Schumacher, who, in 1968, wrote in his essay, "The New Economics":

"In the poor countries in particular there is no hope for the poor unless there is successful regional development, a development effort outside the capital city covering all the rural areas wherever people happen to be.

If this effort is not brought forth, their only choice is either to remain in their miserable condition where they are, or to migrate into the big city where their condition will be even more miserable. It is a strange phenomenon indeed that the conventional wisdom of present-day economics can do nothing to help the poor.

The economic calculus, as applied by present-day economics, forces the industrialist to eliminate the human factor because machines do not make mistakes while people do. Hence the enormous efforts at automation and the drive for ever-larger units. This means that those who have nothing to sell but their labor remain in the weakest possible bargaining position. The conventional wisdom of what is now taught as economics bypasses the poor, the very people for whom development is really needed."

Schumacher's warned of the deleterious consequences of industrialisation driven with a concept of 'productivity', fuelled by technology, that eliminates human beings from the production process. Its effects are being felt today even in the West. He wrote, in his essay on 'Industrialisation through Intermediate Technology':

"If we define the level of technology in terms of 'equipment cost per workplace', we can call the indigenous technology of a typical 'developing' country (symbolically speaking) a $1-techonolgy, while that of the modern West could be called a $1000-technology. The current attempt of the modern West, supported by foreign aid (and investment), to infiltrate the $1000-technology into their economies inevitably kills off the $1-technology at an alarming rate, destroying traditional workplaces much faster than modern workplaces can be created and producing the 'dual economy' with its attendant evils of mass unemployment and mass migration".

Schumacher was drawn towards non-Western concepts of economics. He applied principles of 'Buddhist Economics' to suggest a new economics for the world. He was greatly drawn towards the ideas that Mahatma Gandhi, along with economists around him such as J.C. Kumurappa (sometimes referred to as Gandhi's planning commission), was applying in practice to create new institutions. They designed institutions for a 'peoples' capitalism'—institutions run by, and also owned by, people in villages, in which they could create wealth for themselves rather than for remote capitalists in big cities and in other countries.

The 3% and the 97%

The Covid-19 global pandemic has turned out to be a global catastrophe. Millions of people everywhere have lost their sources of incomes and businesses have collapsed. Economists cannot even predict in what form the economy will emerge. Yet, Wall Street had its biggest 50-day rally in history in the midst of the lock-down!

Twenty years ago, India was shining, according to the government in power then. R.K. Laxman, the cartoonist, had something to say on behalf of 'the common man'. Amidst the headlines of the booming stock market, his cartoon showed two beggars at the bottom of the stairs to the Bombay Stock Exchange. Three stockbrokers are coming down the stairs, laughing. "Oh good. The stock market must have gone up. Now life will be good for us too", says one beggar to the other. In another cartoon, the beggars are looking into a newspaper, whose headline says the GDP has gone up and they don't seem to know what to make of it.

The stock market is not the economy, Noble Laureate economist Paul Krugman stresses. Stocks don't care about your feelings, says an article in the New York Times. Someone on TikTok says that stock prices are a graph of rich people's feelings!

Less than 3% of Indian citizens have investments in the stock market. Stock markets, the judgements of rating agencies, and even GDP, do not represent the realities of the lives of 97% of Indian citizens. In India, while the 3% were celebrating the growth of economies, watching the GDP and stock indices, the twin evils of unemployment and mass migration were growing outside the walls of their physically, and mentally, gated communities. When a lock-down was declared to prevent contagion from the virus, these evils in the economy could not be hidden any longer.

I live in a 5-star apartment complex in India's National Capital Region, with a golf course, a swimming pool, and even a beauty salon on its premises. We are served here by hundreds of workers, inside the gated walls of our community and as domestic help in our homes. They live somewhere outside our walls; we do not know how they live, nor seem to care. When the pandemic broke, migrations began. Wealthy globe-trotters—'people like us'—flew back from wherever they were in the world, for safety in gated condominiums in India. Meanwhile, those who served 'people like us' began their migrations to their villages, many starving and dying on the way, killed not by the virus but by the injustice of the system.

People like us sometimes complained about these, the other Indians, who were not like us. That they were 'not good enough for us' when we employed them in our factories and our homes—too unproductive, and with shoddy habits too. It was something about the 'Indian culture' we would lament—a culture which existed out there, beyond our walls, and not inside our homes. We were alright; they were not.

One morning I ventured, with my mask on, to the small grocery story within our complex, which had valiantly continued to operate, supplying us unfailingly with our essentials. Though some complained that it once in a while had run out of their favourite brand of shampoo. There, while maintaining my social distance from the cashier and the domestic worker who had come down from his apartment to pick up cereals and shampoos for his employers, I overheard this conversation.

The cashier and the domestic worker compared notes. Both were from Bihar, from where they had come with many others seeking a better future for themselves. They inquired about their acquaintances. How were they doing? How many had returned? What news about where they had reached? They exchanged stories of hardships. The domestic worker said his employer had just returned from abroad. "These people travel all over the world", he observed. "Now they have brought the virus to us. And we must leave to look for safety in our villages. No food on the way." Sadly, he seemed resigned to his fate.

While we, who are within the elite 3%, often complain that 'these people are not good enough for us', over-hearing the conversation amongst these two, who were well within the remaining 97%, I felt compelled to ask myself, *"Are we (and our ideas of economics) good for them—these, our own people?"*

A New Dawning

Perhaps the ideas of Gandhiji and his advisers, that were set aside all through the Nehruvian era, the post 1970s socialist era, and the post 1991 liberal era, should stimulate new thinking: not to take India back, but as an impetus for new thinking for India to go forward. The principles apply very well even in the 21st century. New technologies make it even easier now to create enterprises of the people, by the people, for the people than it was in Gandhiji's times.

Whether migrants or not, all Indian citizens are entitled to what India's Constitution promises—'equality of status and opportunity;' 'fraternity assuring the dignity of the individual'; and 'justice—political, social, and economic too'. The migrant crisis has revealed that the old economics—whether the pre-1991 socialist economics, or the post-1991 liberal economics, could not deliver what the Indian Constitution had promised all India's citizens. It is imperative that Indian leaders and economists, who are concerned about India's future, set aside their ideological squabbles, and outline a 'new economics' for India, to enable all Indians to live in dignity, and with adequate economic security, wherever they choose to live; and whether they are migrants from one state to another, migrants from villages to cities, or from cities to villages as millions are now.

The Overton window (named after political scientist Joseph P. Overton) is a model for understanding how ideas in society change over time and influence politics. The window opens when ideas that were on the fringe gain broader relevance. People who have been physically locked-in by the virus, are breaking out in conversations with each other on the internet.

Webinars have become another virus to avoid, some now complain! New ideas about a new, humanistic paradigm of progress, are breaking out of the global financial paradigm whose sell-by date seems to have passed. Many of these conversations that are amongst civil society organizations and amongst gatherings of young people who are determined to build a better India. Such conversations are even beginning to appear amongst financial economists, business leaders, and market traders, who have been most benefitted by, and therefore most vested in, the old paradigm.

GDP, the economists' measure of the size of a nation's economy, must be replaced by more humanistic measures of the economy's health and citizen's well-being. Public policies must focus much more on the needs of the most vulnerable who want to live and earn with dignity, rather than focusing excessively on making it easier for investors to do business and increase their wealth, with the hope that enough of it will trickle down, and much faster too so that the people at the bottom are never shut out again.

Paradigms change when new voices with new ideas enter the public discourse. Through the end of the Covid tunnel, with the Overton window opening wider, I can see the shape of a new economy more clearly. An economy which must be more resilient and more just; more local than global; more community than market. An economy in which humans are humbler about their place within the natural environment that nurtures them.

The time has come to reinvent economics. And to recouple economics with society, to bring Davos down to the people on earth.

(Published by Founding Fuel in June 2020)

C. TECHNOLOGY AND BUSINESS

1

Will Technology Destroy Democracy?

Part 1: The Challenges

We are living in 'interesting times', as the Chinese say, with many global challenges. Geo-politics has heated up again, having cooled off a bit after the collapse of the Soviet Union 30 years ago. Forces of populism and authoritarianism are rising in many parts of the world creating concern among liberals about the future of democracy. Terrorism of many sorts, and with many causes, is striking in many places. In a world where the slow growth of jobs and increasing inequalities have been fuelling social unrest, rapid advances in automation and artificial intelligence (AI) technologies are causing greater anxieties.

Technology is being implicated, indirectly and directly, for these global problems. Job destruction is one of the major problems attributed to technology. The spread of fake news and hatred on social media is another. The wise solution is not to stop the development of new technologies, but to understand how they can be used and misused and to regulate them. Indeed, all new technologies with immense potential have been regulated to prevent them from causing harm: nuclear power, electricity, chemicals, new medicines, etc. Technologies are developed by humans. They are used by humans. And humans must harness them to produce the best outcomes for humans.

Technology and Jobs

First, consider the bundle of technologies that, it is feared, will cause large-scale destruction of jobs—robots, AI, 3-D printers, etc.—collectively bundled into 'Industry 4.0'. The anticipation of its consequences, and the preparation for it, has become a multi-billion-dollar consulting industry.

Governments in developed and developing countries are being advised to develop strategies. It seems they may be sold medicines for a disease they may get in the future, when they should be diagnosing the disease they already have, of slow job growth in their economies even before these technologies have spread.

The recent report from the World Bank, *Trouble in the Making?* says that the impact of these new technologies may have been exaggerated. It estimates that technology will eliminate less than 8% of present jobs in any country in the foreseeable future. Therefore, governments should be focused on why jobs are not being created now, to understand the mix of forces which is creating so-called 'jobless growth', of which technology is only one. A joint report by Ficci and Nasscom on *The Future of Jobs in India-2022*, prepared by EY, says that, whereas new technologies will be disruptive for the IT/IT enabled services (ITES), retail and financial services sectors, their effect on sectors such as apparel, textiles, leather, etc. which are the primary sources of jobs in India, will be relatively marginal in the short term.

'Sewbots' developed by SoftWear Automation, based in Atlanta, US, can replace human beings in sewing apparel. Sewbots can make simple items like pillow cases and bath mats. A sewbot will be able, as soon as next year, to tailor a T-shirt. However, this will not reduce jobs in garment factories in Bangladesh, says Palinaswamy Rajan, the firm's founder. While a sewbot can produce 17 times the number of T-shirts a traditional garment worker can, it may not be economically sensible to replace cheap Bangladeshi labour with expensive sewbots. Rajan says that sewbots will automate only 20-25% of the garment industry even 20-25 years in the future.

Why is India not creating more jobs in apparels and textiles, industries in which it should have competitive advantages? A special report in *The Economist* on premature de-industrialisation in emerging markets, suggests many causes, including poor logistics, and an import policy to protect some Indian manufacturers that raises the cost of man-made fibres which are the principal staples of the global textile and apparels business. The point is, all governments, including India's, must look inwards into the condition of their economies and their policies and improve them before they rush to strategies to cope with Industry 4.0 which providers of technology would love to sell them.

Technology and Democracy

'Will technology destroy democracy?' was an alarming question this year at Forum 2000, the annual conference in Prague, founded 21 years ago by Vaclav Havel, the visionary leader of the Prague Spring and the Velvet Revolution that began the fall of the Soviet Union. The internet and social media were expected to be liberating forces. They enabled the Arab Spring in 2008. Which turned too soon to winter again with a return of authoritarian forces. The internet and social media are tools, like all technologies are, that can be used by both sides: those who oppose and those who defend; for good and for evil.

The internet and social media have the potential, theoretically, to bring the whole world together by enabling people anywhere to reach out to people everywhere. However, the world of social media is not a harmonious world. It is forcing people into tribes of common, often very visceral interests. Because it is practically impossible for a human mind to pay attention to everything, we are compelled to choose what we will follow and what we must ignore. Indeed, walls around 'people like us' have become higher with the spread of social media. People throw hate bombs over the walls. They shout at, and they do not listen at all to those on the other side.

A hundred years ago, long before the invention of social media, Rabindranath Tagore had feared that 'a world broken up into fragments by narrow domestic walls' would not be a world of freedom, in 'which the mind would be without fear and the head could be held high'. Walls between nations are rising again in the new millennium. And walls within nations too, between people of different religions and different cultures. The internet and social media are not the primal causes of peoples' dissatisfactions and fears. However, they have become accelerators.

The speed with which communication technology operates now is causing 'the clear stream of reason to lose its way in the dreary desert sand of dead habit', quoting Tagore again. We must think fast and act fast to keep up with the barrage of information thrust upon us. Algorithms developed by technologists direct our minds to more of what we have indicated we like. Thus, they harden the 'dead habits'—the stereotypes, and the unthinking responses of our minds. The 'thinking fast', instinctual portion of our minds (as Noble Laureate economist Daniel Kahneman called them) is used more, and the 'thinking slow', reflective portion less. In fact, neuro-psychologists are observing measurable changes in the brain structures of children who have become active users of internet and social media compared with brain structures of children two decades ago. They can multi-task and respond to stimuli faster and they may be reflecting less.

The thinking fast portion of all animals' (including human beings) minds helps them to decide very quickly whether to fight or to flee. Whereas the thinking slow portion accepts questions to which there are no immediate answers and it enables reflection. The 'thinking slow' part of our minds makes us pause to look behind the stereotype into the actual reality. Empathy—the ability to put oneself in another's shoes—can arise when we pause and reflect. Therefore, not surprisingly, social scientists have observed a 40% decline in the last ten years in markers of empathy in college students in the USA who are active users of social media. Estimates of how much less time students are spending in the physical company of others range in some surveys from 40% to 80%. Moreover, when they are together, they are very likely to be 'alone together', looking into their smartphones, rather than at each other. They are connected to someone other somewhere else.

Will democracy regulate technology?

Technology has the power to make the world better. It also has the power to make it unsafe. Therefore, powerful technologies must not be allowed to fall into the wrong hands and their use must be regulated. Just as nuclear energy, powerful chemicals, and new medicines are regulated, rapidly developing communication, computational, and AI technologies will have to be regulated too.

Democracy demands that human beings (and all of them equally), should be able to determine the rules by which they will be governed. Those who own technologies have great incentives to monopolise their use and prevent others from using them. The incentives can be financial, as they are with intellectual property. Hence the expensive legal battles between companies, and the emerging trade battles about intellectual property between rich and poorer countries. Or the incentive to own the technology can be security, as it is with nuclear weapons. Whereas there must be regulation, those who have the power to make the rules will make rules that preserve their power. Which is not democratic.

Democratic deliberation requires that everyone has an equal voice. Moreover, since the global problems humanity is being challenged by in these 'interesting times' are complex, many points of view must be combined to understand their causes and to find sustainable solutions. Therefore, people must listen to each other, across the walls that divide them, and understand each other's perspectives. More reflective conversations are necessary among people who are not like each other and may not even like each other. Whereas social media is making listening across the walls harder, not easier.

Part 2: How to Find Solutions? Who Will Regulate Technology?

The premise of democracy is that the regulations that govern citizens are developed by a democratic process in which they can participate. Democratic governments are elected by people within defined boundaries. All the people within those boundaries must elect their government. Governments cannot have jurisdiction over people outside those boundaries who have not participated in the election of the government. Of course, if the people within those boundaries are not free to elect their own government, either because they are ruled by an autocratic, non-elected government, or if they are a colony of another country, there is no democracy (even if the 'colonising' country has a democratically elected government).

It follows from this premise that citizens must have a right to determine the policies that will govern the use of technology in their country. Even if the country's government is not democratically elected, another country cannot impose its policies on it for that would not be democratic.

Citizens have many expectations from their governments, whether democratically elected or not. They expect that a good government will create conditions for them to obtain what they need to live good lives—decent jobs with adequate incomes, adequate housing and infrastructure, and good social services for health and education, etc. They would also expect their government to ensure their safety from external or internal threats. And they would prefer that their government gives them liberty, freedom of expression, and the right to criticise their government too, which are the visible markers of democracies.

Tolstoy said, "Happy families are all alike; every unhappy family is unhappy in its own way." People in all countries want to have even better conditions for themselves and for their children and grandchildren. That is the path to progress. However, countries are at different places along the path, and may be even on different paths towards a better future. Therefore, the mix of what citizens of each country need for progress is different. Some may value greater economic security now and a stronger government to deliver it. Others may want more liberty now. Indeed, the rise of populism in the West is an indication that people have requirements that even democratic governments were not fulfilling.

Like Tolstoy's unhappy families, unhappy in their own ways, countries will need policies and mechanisms to regulate technology that fit their requirements. One-size-fits-all solutions will not be appropriate. Champions of democracy must encourage the development of solutions with the participation of stakeholders within countries. The test of democracy's strength must be the engagement of stakeholders *within* countries. Imposition of solutions developed by experts, from outside or within the country, would be undemocratic.

With increasing globalisation of finance and trade since the 1970s, and with it the increasing power of corporations who want freedom to be anywhere, and whose loyalty does not lie with any country, a parallel world of global governance had grown. In this parallel world, sometimes called the 'Davos world', leaders of governments, large multi-national corporations, and economists evangelising globalisation, were seen to be actively consulting each other. The agenda on the mountain top was to develop policies for providing more freedom for capital and investors. On the ground, in many countries, citizens began to feel disconnected with the global elite. Their alienation from the elites' agenda has spurred the rise of populist, and nationalist, political forces.

Who should be trusted to regulate the use of internet and social media technologies that have great power over citizens' minds? Can governments be trusted by their citizens? Or, can owners of the companies, sitting in some other country, that make money from these technologies, be trusted more? It is also an ideological issue: more private enterprise and less government, or more socialism? It is a practical issue too: how will the regulations be enforced? Can corporations be freed from regulation by national governments and trusted to regulate themselves?

The quality of the dialogues will determine the quality of the regulations.

Dialogues about what citizens' needs are, and what sort of regulations of technology they will support, are necessary for democratic solutions. Such dialogues must be not only among private business and government leaders. They must include civil society. Many points of view must be considered. No doubt, ideologies will complicate these deliberations, as well as defenses of vested interests. Therefore, the quality of the dialogues will determine the quality of the regulations.

The consensus at Forum 2000 was that the democratic conversations which have become necessary to determine how to sensibly regulate the use of new, digital, computational and communication technologies will have to be conducted 'offline', in old-fashioned, analogue formats. People must switch off their smartphones and online chatter; and learn to switch off the chatter of dead habits in their minds. We must pause and listen to other points of view. We must learn to reflect together on the shape of the elephants in the room that will emerge when we combine our perspectives and think systemically.

Without listening, the clear stream of reason is lost in the dreary desert sand of dead habits

Listening is the first of the three wisdom tools in Buddhist tradition, His Holiness the Dalai Lama says in his Foreword to my book, *Listening for Well-Being: Conversations with People Not Like Us* The other two are contemplating and meditating. If one listens deeply, one can learn something new, about the world and about other people, that is not already in one's mind. From listening comes something to contemplate and to understand. Without listening, the clear stream of reason is lost in the dreary desert sand of dead habits. And the world is broken into fragments, as Tagore warned.

The skills of communication taught in schools and leadership programmes are oriented heavily towards how to get one's point of view across forcefully, in inspiring speeches, in debates, and in tweets. Skills for the other side of communication, for listening, are hardly taught. When everyone is shouting and tweeting, there is only a cacophony. There is no communication. There is no understanding. There is no wisdom.

The conclusion is that the technology most urgently required to develop better regulations of technology democratically, is improvement and application of an old-fashioned technology of dialogue with deep listening to many points of view to find solutions that will be fair for all. Listening to and dialogue with people not like us will also strengthen democracy.

(Published by Founding Fuel in October 2017)

2

A Business Redesign to Make Capitalism More Inclusive

The number of millionaires at the top of India's economy is growing while millions are scrambling for employment to earn adequate incomes. Something is missing in the middle of the economy.

The concept of a "circular economy" is being promoted to sustain the environment. It shows how materials and energy flow through production systems. It is a way to map and manage all material resources through their life cycle so that nothing is wasted. Another view of a circular economy explains how wealth is generated and flows through the economy. It reveals missing middles in India's economic structure.

C. K. Prahalad promulgated the concept of "the fortune at the bottom of the pyramid". He used an example of the shampoo sachet to explain it. A multinational company wanted to sell its shampoo to poor people who could not afford to buy a whole bottle of shampoo. So, it repackaged its shampoo in very small sachets that could be purchased by people with little money. That way, poor people could get the benefit of a good product for hair hygiene, which they could not afford earlier. This is good "Business For the People".

But providing people with affordable products does not address the root cause of poverty. People are poor because they do not have incomes. They need employment and incomes to lift themselves out of poverty. Therefore, they must be engaged in the processes of producing goods and services. The economy needs innovations in business models that provide more jobs, so that business is not only "For the People" but "By the People" too.

By packaging its shampoo in small sachets, the company was able to increase its sales. However, the profit from the expansion of shampoo sales went to investors in the company wherever they were in the world. They made the profits, not the people. The wealth of investors increased further: they had found another fortune at the bottom of the pyramid.

The issue, therefore, is: who owns the enterprise? The people at the bottom, or people at the top of the economy? Unless people who work become the owners of the enterprises, they will not be making any profits, nor will they earn wealth. Those who have wealth will make more wealth by investing it in more enterprises to make more profits. Those who have little wealth, or none at all, will be left further behind. Therefore, we need enterprises run by the people and owned by the people too if we want to reduce income and wealth disparities.

There are similarities in the structures of the circular material economy and the circular financial economy. In the material economy, solid waste is generated from the production system and it begins to accumulate in a few places, choking up rivers and oceans. In the financial economy, financial capital is generated out of the production system and it accumulates in the financial sector.

The size of the financial sector in all economies has grown greatly in the past 30 years. Financial resources from banking are being invested in financial funds—in hedge funds, derivatives, etc. There they create more financial wealth for investors. They do not go back into the production sector. The size of the financial sector of economies has been increasing. In the US, for example, from 1960 to 2014, finance's share of gross value added more than doubled from 3.7% to 8.4%, while manufacturing's share more than halved from 25% to 12%. At the same time, only 15% of the funds generated are going to businesses in non-financial industries, says Rana Foroohar in *Makers And Takers* (2016). In India too, while stock markets boom, sufficient investments are not going to the manufacturing sector, which can provide more productive jobs.

Just as the environmental system is getting choked by solid waste, the shift in the structure of capitalist economies to financial capitalism is now choking up the economic system with the accumulation of a virtual resource, i.e. money.

Employees of enterprises owned by others can have incomes, but cannot share in the creation of wealth, the fruits of which go entirely to their capitalist owners. For fuller inclusion in the benefits of growth, innovations are required in enterprise design by which the producers become owners too. Such are enterprises and businesses "Of the People". In this vision, India, a country of over a billion democrats, can also be a country with hundreds of millions of capitalists spread throughout the economic pyramid.

The concept of "Businesses Of the people" is not new. They operate in many countries, including in India, with examples such as the Amul dairy cooperative, the SEWA group of women's enterprises, and other examples of weavers' and farmers' cooperatives. This strand of capitalism must be strengthened to fill the missing middle in India's economic structure and make capitalism more inclusive.

Why are there too few such enterprises in India even though there are some good examples? Management schools do not teach methods for building cooperative enterprises. These enterprises are encumbered by regulations which make expansion difficult. But more importantly, because it is not an aspirational idea of a strong economy: It is too "Gandhian", not Wall Street.

Businesses For, By and Of the People will make capitalism more democratic.

(Published by Mint in May 2019)

3

'Shares' versus 'Values' Conflict in Business

The Covid pandemic has highlighted the urgency for economists to find a 'new normal' economics, which they have been searching for ever since the global financial crisis proved that the old economics was not working. Even before the financial crisis, the Edelman Trust Barometer, a global survey, had revealed that people were losing trust in business corporations.

This month, the US Congress hauled up CEOs of social media companies — the new corporate giants — for social irresponsibility. Clearly, businesses cannot carry on the way they are. They must become accountable to society.

Therefore, it is surprising when Raghuram Rajan, a greatly admired economist in India and elsewhere too, writes "Shareholder value isn't past its sell-by date as a corporate goal" (@2020 project syndicate). Rajan says The Business Roundtable, a group of the largest US corporations, was misguided to 'respond to the public mood', to declare, 'Each of our stakeholders is essential. We commit to deliver value to all of them.'

Exactly 50 years ago, in September 1970, Milton Friedman, the Noble Laureate economist, wrote in *The New York Times* that the business of business must be only to make profits for its shareholders. Friedman was the most prominent thought-leader of the Chicago School of Economics; Rajan teaches in the same university.

Rajan says, "If companies want to maximise their shares' value, they will train workers, and encourage sustainable practices from the suppliers". The evidence, however, is that they don't. When focussed only on their own profits and share price, they treat society and the environment as 'externalities', the harm to which is not deducted from their profits.

A good management principle is that you can manage only what you measure. Therefore, if you measure only profits and share values, that is only what will be managed. Responding to pressure from the public, and to their own consciences too, many business leaders have voluntarily developed comprehensive scorecards, such as the Global Reporting Initiative, the UN Global Compact, and (in India), the National Voluntary Guidelines. Rajan implies this is wrong-headed, and businesses should return to the Chicago doctrine of focussing on the measurement of shareholder value.

Ideas are hard to change, Thomas Kuhn explained in *The Structure of Scientific Revolutions*. An ecosystem of vested interests builds around an idea, and the idea then becomes a 'paradigm'. Thus, a large network of interlocked industries has grown around the use of fossil fuels: coal and oil producers, power companies, vehicles powered by internal combustion engines, and countries with large fossil fuel resources. This system will resist the shift to de-fossilisation to slow climate change.

A large industry has grown around the idea of shareholder value — investors, stock markets, financial analysts, venture capitalists, and economists who provide them intellectual ammunition. The enormous wealth created in this 'de-materialised' industry in the last thirty years has resulted in huge inequalities in wealth, between those who work and live in the 'real' economy, and those who operate in this world of virtual wealth. CEOs who want to change the world from within, like The Business Roundtable, are being pushed back by the system around them.

Two Tenets

The economics and management paradigm that has become normal in the last 50 years is based on two tenets. The first is the wrong belief that all human beings are rational, self-interested economic agents. Business corporations are run on the same principle when their managers are charged to look after the interests of their own corporations' shareholders. In a world filled with only selfish agents, economists say that the care of the common good is produced by the operation of an invisible hand. These 'rational' economists ignore the evidence around them. Humans are social and emotional animals. They even befriend other species — horses, dogs, cats, and cows, often quite irrationally.

The second tenet is the imperative to 'focus'. As Rajan says, 'if all stakeholders are essential, then none are'. Mothers care for all their children, no matter how many they have. They do not say, because I have two, I cannot care for either of them! The SDGs (Sustainable Development Goals) require that many things must be kept in mind and improved together — the economy, the environment, and the conditions of people's lives.

Surely no economist, or CEO, in the 21st century should say that he will focus only on the condition of the business and not on the condition of people's lives, or only on the condition of the economy and not on the condition of the environment. Managers must learn to manage with 'all things considered'. And economists must develop better scorecards of societal well-being than the singular GDP measure they have become addicted to.

The present normal of management, with governments broken into silos of ministries and international development agencies broken into silos of specialists, cannot find solutions to the systemic problems that the SDGs have made vivid. Policy makers, economists, and CEOs must apply 'systems thinking' to improve the well-being of societies. They must listen to many points of view to understand the whole system of which they are only a small part.

Economist Albert Hirschman saw the contradiction between institutions of capitalism and democracy building up 50 years ago. He pointed out, in his book *Exit, Voice, and Loyalty,* that Milton Friedman had expressed his difficulty in accepting the notion that people should desire to express their views to make them prevail. Friedman described this as a resort to 'cumbrous political channels'. He would much rather people resort to 'efficient market mechanisms' and use their money rather than their mouths to make their opinions known.

But what if people have little money, or no money? How can they influence reforms to make them just for poor people and less harmful for the environment? The time has come for economists and business leaders to listen to the voices of people and not only to the voices of money speaking.

The sell-by date of 'the business of business is only business' has indeed passed.

(Published by The Hindu Business Line in October 2020)

4

Some Questions About the Ugly Side of Charity

The UK Charity Commissioner has published a scathing report following its investigation of complaints of sexual harassment by Oxfam's aid workers in Haiti. Oxfam has also revealed the critical findings of an independent report it had commissioned. Almost everything in these reports could be written about many international NGOs because the issues are systemic across the aid sector. They arise from the fundamental values that pervade philanthropic organisations and even government aid programmes. Power corrupts and even power to do good can corrupt.

The first question is the purpose of the charitable enterprise. Is it to provide humanitarian aid or development assistance? The objective of humanitarian aid is to give assistance to people in distress caused by natural calamities, political upheavals or perennial poverty. It provides flows of material assistance from those who are fortunate to those who are in need. On the other hand, the purpose of development assistance is to help those who are not yet able to provide for themselves to be able to do so as soon as possible. The dichotomy between relief of distress and the development of capabilities runs through the NGO sector. It also runs through government programmes: writing off the debts of farmers versus enabling them to earn more or providing universal basic income via cash transfers when people can't earn enough versus changing the system so that people have jobs and earn more.

Charity is primarily a one-way flow of assistance from donors to beneficiaries, but capabilities are developed by sensitive partnerships. Programmes of NGOs and governments, whose primary purpose is charity and humanitarian relief, can be improved with tools of business management to make delivery systems efficient, optimise use of resources and "create more value for money". The drive for more efficiency in deliveries of services by NGOs and governments has led to greater engagements of management consultants by them over the last 20 years. This makes NGOs and governments more "business-like" and enables them to attract more money from capitalists who understand quantifiable concepts of efficiency and returns more than fuzzy, "socialist" ideas of equity.

Changing a complex system's structure so that it will not have holes is much harder than merely filling the holes. It is even more difficult to modify an existing building to eliminate the causes of the holes when people are already living in it. Vested power structures must be sensitively taken into account while making changes, like the load-supporting beams in an old structure, or the whole house could collapse. Business management concepts of innovation and design are primarily geared to finding missing holes in the system i.e. unmet needs for which a new product or app can be designed and efficiently delivered. Society expects business managers to produce more profits for investors, not to make the world more just—"the business of business must be only business"—whereas the mission of good governments, and good development NGOs, must be to make the world better and more equitable. Thus, prevalent business management toolkits are inadequate, perhaps even inappropriate for development work.

Academic experts in economics and social development use their research tools with people as data to devise solutions to "solve poverty" which will impress other academicians and also policymakers. The experts want to administer prescriptions for poor people. Dr Abhay Bang, who has won global acclaim for path-breaking work in public health work that his wife Rani and he have done in one of India's poorest districts, points out that researchers apply their skills to do research for their peers, not for the community. They do research "on the people", rather than research "for and with the people".

A fundamental difference between charity and genuine developmental support, such as Rani and Abhay Bang have provided to the people in Gadchiroli for decades, is the relationship between providers and beneficiaries. Charity flows from patrons with wealth and power, while good development partners are "allies" who work alongside.

The UK Charity Commission's report ends with an admonishment that "charities must never lose sight of why they exist and must demonstrate how their charitable purpose drives everything they do". It alludes to the conundrum of the purpose of the enterprise that I began with—is it humanitarian aid and charity, or partnership for development? Deborah Doane, commenting on the Commission's report in The Guardian (12 June 2019), says that the charitable aid system is built on a power imbalance. "Money and power are the cornerstones of exploitation and rich donors have both," she says.

People listen to money and power: money and power do not listen to people. In *Winners Take All: The Elite Charade Of Changing The World*, Anand Giridharadas explains how money and power, and the egos that grow with them, shape ideas ruling the worlds of philanthropy and charity. Even among NGOs, those who have bigger budgets and brands, and whose practices have been shaped by good business management precepts, are considered leaders; rather than the un-business-like precepts of Rani and Abhay Bhang's tiny organization "of the people, by the people, for the people" in Gadchiroli. In the world of development, small can be more effective and beautiful too.

(Published by Mint June 2019)

5

Gandhi not Milton Friedman

Upon winning the elections, Prime Minister Modi has declared, with one of his usual flourishes, that the era of caste-based politics is over. From now on there will be only two castes, he says: those who are poor and those who want to free them from poverty. Some economists are fearing the country is slipping back into socialism. They are urging Mr. Modi to take advantage of his renewed mandate to minimize government. They should introspect on their own responsibilities as members of the caste that must reduce poverty and examine if their tools are designed for the task.

The government, NGOs, and businesses belong to the caste that must free people from poverty. The government's dharma in a country with millions of poor people has to be to free the poor from poverty. NGOs are devoted to helping less-well off citizens in various ways. Businesses too, are taking interest in uplifting the poor, through philanthropy, CSR, and new forms of social business ventures. This caste, of government, NGOs, and businesses, needs a new tool-kit to have a greater impact in its mission to reduce poverty. The tool-kit it is applying is increasingly being adopted from the world of business. It is not the appropriate tool-kit for the task of reducing poverty sustainably.

The collapse of the Soviet Union marked a landmark in the history of ideologies, noted by Francis Fukuyama in his book, 'The End of History and the Last Man'. The ideologies of free markets and capitalism had defeated forever the ideas of communism and socialism for the governance of societies, he said. Ronald Regan and Margret Thatcher were the heroes of an Anglo-Saxon model of capitalism, and Milton Friedman, a Noble Laureate in economics, was their intellectual guide. Ronald Regan declared that 'government is not the solution; it is the problem'. Friedman, while favoring business over government, went further to say that 'the business of business must only be business'.

Admiration of business management methods, and demands for its purveyors, i.e. business management schools and business management consultants, has greatly increased in the last thirty years, since the moment history ended according to Fukuyama. Leaders of governments were urged to perform like CEOs of large business corporations, even to appear with their report-cards before the leaders of the business world in Davos. Business management consultants were hired to reform governments. Large NGOs, who can afford to, also hire management consultants to guide them.

Five years ago, when he first became Prime Minister of India, Mr. Modi had coined the phrase, 'Minimum Government, Maximum Governance'. Economists of the Regan-Thatcher tradition, noting the first half of his slogan, cheered him. They were dismayed when he did not reduce the government's role in the economy. He seemed more focused on the second half, of maximum governance from the perspective of the poor, as he should be as a leader democratically elected by hundreds of millions of people not completely out of poverty. Thus, he won the people's trust and they re-elected him with a larger majority.

The ideology of business, since Friedman, is that the purpose of a business is to increase returns for its financial investors. The management took-kit that business' use provides methods for increasing efficiency and profits. It includes lenses to find more opportunities to make profits—including profits from the 'bottom of the pyramid' by devising new products and services the poor need and can pay for. Within this world-view it would be immoral of a manager to give away something, that ultimately belongs to financial shareholders, to someone who cannot afford to pay for it. Therefore, those who cannot afford to pay for the healthcare and medicines the business is selling, perforce must be excluded from the scope of the business. The business of business must be business; it cannot be charity and provision of free services to the poor. Equity amongst citizens, which must be the prime concern of a democratic government, is not the concern of a business.

In the paradigm of maximizing share-holder value, value must be extracted for shareholders from customers, the physical environment and from society. More powerful analytical tools can reveal which customer segments produce least profits, which employees are least efficient, and which environmental resources have the most potential for profit. Rigorous quantification, aided by more powerful computation tools, drives non-quantifiable values out from management equations, such as injustice in the use of a community's resources, and the impacts of a company's practices on the lives of its employees and their families. These are incalculable 'externalities' to the business model.

The dominant paradigm of business management of shareholder value maximization would presume that was is good for the business' shareholders must be good for everyone; that others benefit from the operation of some 'invisible hand'. This selfish paradigm has caused a decline in citizens' trust in businesses around the world. The mistrust is erupting in the US in a revival of 'socialist' ideas which worries hard-core capitalists. Therefore, it is ironical that, in much poorer India, some economists and business leaders should be urging the government to convince the masses that more big business and less government is good for them!

Doctor heal thyself. Rather than crying for less government, business should improve its own governance. And It should re-design its management tool-kit before teaching it to governments and NGOs.

Role models must be chosen carefully. The policies of Franklin D. Roosevelt, and ideas of John Maynard Keynes, which grew an inclusive US economy after a great depression, with a universal social security system and government investments stimulating growth, are better models for India's needs today than the 'minimum government' ideas of Ronald Regan and Milton Friedman. It would be wise to also recall President Dwight D. Eisenhower's caution: "Should any political party attempt to abolish social security, unemployment insurance, eliminate labor laws and farm programs, you would not hear of that party again in our political history". If we must import ideas from Washington, let us choose the ones that apply to our conditions today.

The ethics of citizenship in a good society demand that individuals take care of others' needs, not just their own. No individual can be forgiven for harm caused to another while looking after his own needs no matter how desperate. A good citizen is not the one who has the most wealth, but the one who always respects the rights and needs of others.

Corporations are virtual entities that have acquired all the rights of human citizens of societies—the right to own property, the right to free speech, the right to sue, the right to justice in courts. They are giants in size amongst human citizens: some with more wealth than most countries' GDPs. Thus, they have powers that common citizens do not have. Surely it is unethical for these giants to not just surreptitiously follow their own interests, but even declare that their goal is to pursue only their own interest (the business of business being only business)!

Some business leaders have struck out onto a different path—dared to, one may say. Paul Poling, former CEO of Unilever, comes to mind. Poling courageously broke away from the practice of explaining his company's financial performance to analysts every quarter because they would not understand the longer-term objectives he had in mind. However, he could not escape the gravitational pull of the system of institutions which Unilever is locked into—stock markets, market regulators, business analysts, and financial auditors. His legacy is already under scrutiny with questions whether his strategy of sustainability has increased returns to shareholders—the over-riding measure of performance amongst the business-capitalist establishment. Tata Steel, with its century-long record of social responsibility, has struggled against the spread of the ideology that the business of business must be only business. In 2000, by when the company had joined global markets, its CEO was asked by an analyst, during a quarterly earnings call, when the company would stop being 'socialist'!

The Anglo-Saxon system of capitalism is formed around pervasive ideas about the purpose of a business corporation, measures of its performance, and methods for achieving its goals. These ideas and tools are taught in business schools, applied by management consultants, and reinforced by the financial markets. It is not possible for any CEO, or any company alone, to escape the demands of the system. When they step out to create new forms of enterprises, such as 'social ventures', to create social impact, they cannot escape pervasive expectations of financial returns and efficiency from investors.

The history of humanity's progress on multiple fronts shows that it is not enough to have high aspirations; one must also develop vehicles to take one there. The dream to reach the moon could not be realized with airplanes that cannot escape Earth's gravitational pull. Rockets, with very different shapes to airplanes, made it possible.

In Gandhiji's 150th anniversary year, one must remember his vision of a casteless society without poverty. Business leaders should recall Gandhiji's plea to them to be trustees of societies' wealth. And, all leaders in government and business should remember his talisman. "Whenever you are in doubt, or when the self becomes too much with you, apply the following test. Recall the face of the poorest and the weakest man [woman] whom you may have seen, and ask yourself, if the step you contemplate is going to be of any use to him [her]". Clearly this will not be the face of a financial investor in the corporation.

Dominant ideas of business management do not provide an appropriate tool-kit for institutions who aspire to reduce poverty and create an equitable society. Business management itself needs a new, ethical toolkit. It must begin with a redefinition of the purpose of the corporation in society. Which must be the improvement of the well-being of everyone, not just increasing the wealth of investors. Business managers must be re-oriented towards systems thinking, to see their small place within a system shaped by many forces. Business leaders must have more humility and display less arrogance that, because they have accumulated large wealth for themselves, they know better than governments and civil society organizations how to make the world better for everyone.

(Blogpost published June 2019)

Acknowledgements

This book is an outcome of my listening deeply for over twenty years to many diverse people around the world when they talked about their aspirations for a better world for everyone, and they shared ideas about how the world would be improved. I acknowledge the hundreds of inspiring people I met in these gatherings, and I thank the leaders who enabled these meetings to happen.

Tarun Das and N. Srinivasan of the Confederation of Indian Industry supported a process in India in 1999 and 2000, which they invited me to facilitate. Hundreds of diverse people gathered in many meetings, using the methods of 'generative scenario planning'. They included homeless children living on the streets of New Delhi, schoolteachers, business leaders, and economists in India's Planning Commission. Their insights into the forces shaping India, and their vision of a better way for India's development, produced scenarios of India's future which are included in this book.

Graham Leicester and his friends in Scotland convened thought-leaders from around the world, in the International Futures Forum in St. Andrews, where Adam Smith lived and wrote, and which was a birthplace of ideas of the European Enlightenment, that have propelled remarkable scientific advances and economic growth. Concerned about the side-effects of those ideas—the damage to the natural environment, and the inequalities between countries and within them, the International Futures Forum began an ambitious search for a new Enlightenment. I journeyed with them and listened and learned.

Georg Kell, the first CEO of the UN Global Compact founded by UN Secretary General Kofi Annan, invited me to counsel with him as he developed the compact. I participated in many meetings of industry leaders from around the world. I listened to their dialogues with human rights advocates and civil society leaders who challenged the business leaders' views of economies.

Bo Ekman, the inspiring founder of the Tallberg Forum, invited me for many years to the annual gatherings of the Forum in the village of Tallberg on the shores of Lake Siljan in central Sweden. There, hundreds of persons, from all continents of the world, and diverse walks of life—social workers, academics, business leaders, and poets and musicians too—deliberated on the future of humanity.

Ged Davis, Managing Director of the World Economic Forum, and I facilitated the development of scenarios for the future of India in 2005, in an extensive participative process, when the WEF wanted to examine more deeply the likely futures of the BRICS countries, to which the world's attention had then turned.

Dr. Manmohan Singh, Prime Minister of India, and Chairman of India's Planning Commission, and Montek Ahluwalia, its Deputy Chairman, gave me an unusual opportunity to sit with them in the cockpit of India from July 2009 to June 2014 to survey the forces shaping a vast and diverse, and noisily democratic, country of one billion persons. They encouraged me to set up new, more open, processes to listen to citizens to supplement the formal processes of the Planning Commission.

Luke Jordan of the World Bank, who was posted in India at that time, enabled me to visit other countries to learn how their leaders were organizing participatory processes of policymaking and shaping industrial policies. Aart de Geuss and his colleagues in the Bertelsmann Stiftung invited me to dip into their research of how countries are developing policies for sustainable and inclusive growth, and with them I have listened to thought-leaders from many countries.

Dennis Snower, President of the Kiel Institute of the Global Economy, has included me in many meetings of the Global Economic Symposium and the Global Solutions Initiative over the last ten years. In these meetings, Nobel laureates in economics, and thought leaders in other disciplines have debated the changes necessary in their theories. Hundreds of change-makers from many countries have also participated in the discussions with these experts, challenging their orthodox views of good economic science. The theme of the meetings has become the "recoupling of economics with society" which runs through this book.

While I have been listening, I have been writing too. Editors of India's leading newspapers have invited me to write in their pages. I would like to acknowledge some here: Niranjan Rajadhyaksha and Aresh Shirali in the Mint; Rajkamal Jha in the Indian Express; V. Srinivasan in The Hindu; and Jagdish Rattnani of the Billion Press who has placed my articles in the Hindu Business Line and other papers. This book includes some pieces published in their journals.

A special thank you to Indrajit Gupta, Charles Assisi, and Sveta Basraon of Founding Fuel, who gave me space, whenever I wanted it, to speak out on their website, and also helped me to clarify what I was saying. I have included several pieces here which have been published by Founding Fuel.

In the last five years, I have been gifted with conversations with many young leaders who are shaping movements of change in India. They have given me opportunities to meet hundreds more. Sunil Savara and Madan Padaki invited me to curate gatherings of change-makers at the Sabarmati Ashram and Gujarat Vidyapeeth in Ahmedabad—Gandhiji's old haunts. There, builders of large movements of change—Elabhen Bhat, Muhammad Yunus, Aruna Roy, Vijay Mahajan, and others, interacted with hundreds of young people who were taking steps to make differences in the lives of people around them in their villages and towns.

Vineet Rai, founder of the Aavishkar group of social enterprises, and of the Sankalp Forum in which hundreds of social entrepreneurs present their stories, exchange ideas, and develop partnerships, has provided me with note-books full of ideas.

Many young, and older, leaders of movements of change are teaching me now. With them, I am listening to many more inspiring young people in their networks for change. I cannot name all these remarkable leaders: the list will be very long. Some are: Ashok Khosla, Ankit Chhabra, Ashif Khan,

Atul Satija, Harish Hande, Harsh Mander, Hemakshi Meghani, Prakhar Bhartiya, Priya Naik, Raghav Krishna, Reema Nanavati, Renana Jhabwala, Shobhit Mathur, Smarinita Shetty, Shashank Mishra, and Suparna Diwakar. While mentioning only a few, I ask for forgiveness of the others.

I must thank Shama, my life-long companion, most of all, for her encouragement as well as her tolerance. We have been married for fifty-four lovely years now. Till the lock-down grounded me, I was always travelling, according to her, meeting people around the world, and never having enough time with her. In fact, I had bought a new, expensive carry-on bag in March 2020, preparing for three intercontinental trips in the next two months. However, the lock-down was imposed a few days later. The bag has remained in its wrapper.

Since then, I have been home all the time. Thanks to the internet and zoom, I became even busier, meeting many more people than before. My notebooks filled up rapidly. I had more time to write too. Shama complained that she could never have me to herself; she had to make appointments to meet me even though we were locked into the same home! However, she was pleased that I was feeling fulfilled, and looked after me very well while I was meeting more people than before, and while I even wrote five books during the lock-down!

This one, the fourth of the five to be published—the fifth will be published later this year—was very important to get out soon. With vaccines rolling out, and with possibilities of life "going back to normal" again, it is necessary that we must pause and remind ourselves of the resolutions we made during the lock-down that we would *not* go back to normal. My friends in the publishing industry recommended a "new age" publisher who, using the power of technology, could turn this book around very fast. I am grateful to Naveen Valsakumar, founder and CEO of Notionpress, for producing this book so quickly.

I hope it will be read by many people stepping out to make a new world better for everyone. It is a reminder of our resolve; as well as a compendium of ideas that outline solutions and give hope.

www.ingramcontent.com/pod-product-compliance
Lightning Source LLC
Chambersburg PA
CBHW020859180526
45163CB00007B/2558